LAST TRAIN SOUTH

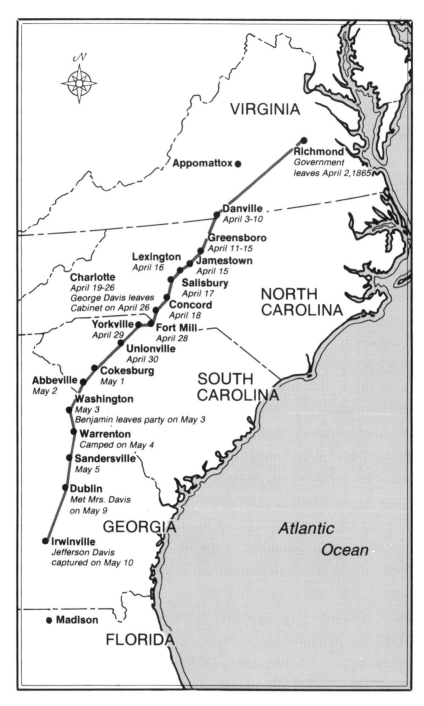

The flight of Jefferson Davis and others (see maps on pages xi–xii).

James C. Clark

LAST TRAIN SOUTH

The Flight of the Confederate Government from Richmond

McFarland & Company, Inc., Publishers   1984
Jefferson, North Carolina, and London

Cover: The Evacuation of Richmond, April 1865. Mayo Bridge. Courtesy Valentine Museum, Richmond

British Library Cataloguing-in-Publication data are available

Library of Congress Cataloguing-in-Publication Data

Clark, James C., 1947–
  Last train south.

    Bibliography: p.
    Includes index.
    1. Richmond (Va.)—Siege, 1864–1865.
  2. Davis, Jefferson, 1808–1889—Captivity, 1865–1867.
  3. Confederate States of America—Politics and government.
  4. United States—History—Civil War, 1861–1865—Campaigns.
  I. Title.
  E477.61.C53   1984   973.7'38   84-42610

  ISBN 0-7864-0469-8 (softcover : 50# alkaline paper)

Manufactured in the United States of America

McFarland & Company, Inc., Publishers
  Box 611, Jefferson, North Carolina 28640

To Randall Healy Clark
and Kevin Healy Clark,
with love

Table of Contents

Contents

Between chapters X and XI are 16 plates containing Confederate portraits, eyewitness sketches, and contemporary photographs

Preface

In most revolutions, the army is the government, and
when the army is defeated, the rebellion ceases to exist. The
Confederate States of America was different; before there was
an army, there was a government with a president, cabinet,
ambassadors and a bureaucracy that usually comes with a
more established government.

But the Confederate government never matched the
bravery or ability of its army. The internal discord of the Confederate government would have been enough to bring down
a more established government, much less a fledgling nation
fighting for its existence.

The Confederate government could not agree on how
to run the war, and it could not agree on how to end the war.
The Confederate Congress knew the cause was lost and left
Richmond quickly before the Union troops closed in, leaving
President Jefferson Davis and his cabinet with the pieces.

This is the story of those final days as confusion mixed

with false hope and led the leaders of the Confederate government to a desperate flight from Richmond. As the North celebrated the surrender of the Army of Northern Virginia at Appomattox Court House, Davis and his cabinet dreamed that somehow victory was still possible.

Their dream carried them through Virginia, North Carolina, South Carolina and into Georgia, but no matter where they went, they came no closer to salvaging the Confederacy.

The flight of the Confederate government lasted just a few weeks, but it demonstrated the false hope which had plagued the Confederacy from the beginning.

Throughout their flight, the members of the Confederate government received assistance from helpful people. Throughout the preparation of this book, the author has received aid from people who gave their time to check facts, provide a worthwhile lead or simply offer moral support.

Sarah Shields, the curator of the Valentine Museum library in Richmond, gave much time as did several people at the museum of the Confederacy. The staffs of the Rollins College Library and manuscript collection of the Library of Congress were generous with their assistance. The editors of *Civil War Times* were unselfish in giving advice and encouragement.

James C. Clark
Summer 1997

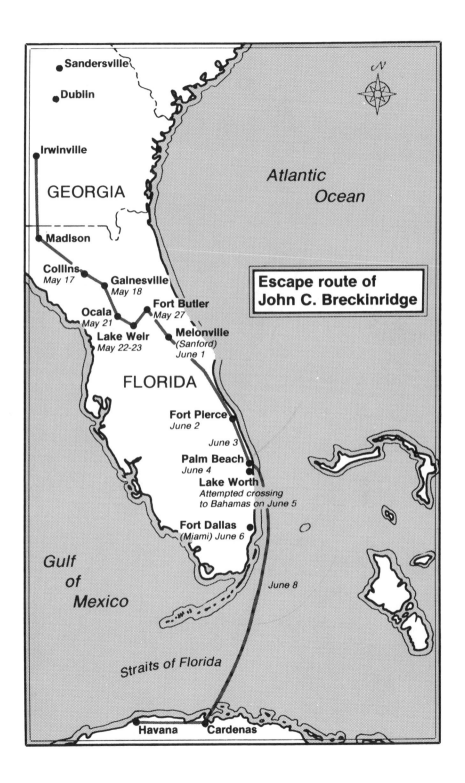

Sandersville

Dublin

Irwinville

GEORGIA

Atlantic
Ocean

Madison

Collins
May 17

Galnesville
May 18

Fort Butler
May 27

Ocala
May 21

Melonville
(Sanford)
June 1

Lake Weir
May 22-23

FLORIDA

**Escape route of
John C. Breckinridge**

Fort Pierce
June 2

June 3

Palm Beach
June 4

Lake Worth
*Attempted crossing
to Bahamas on June 5*

Fort Dallas
(Miami) June 6

Gulf
of
Mexico

June 8

Straits of Florida

Havana   Cardenas

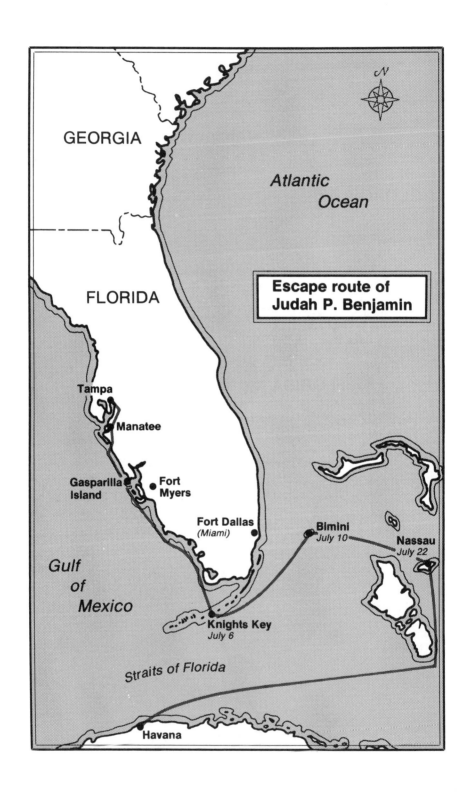

GEORGIA

Atlantic
Ocean

FLORIDA

Escape route of
Judah P. Benjamin

Tampa

Manatee

Gasparilla
island

Fort
Myers

Fort Dallas
(Miami)

Bimini
July 10

Nassau
July 22

Gulf
of
Mexico

Knights Key
July 6

Straits of Florida

Havana

I. The Confederates Leave and Richmond Falls

John C. Breckinridge sat alone in his office on the morning of February 7, 1865, one day after he was sworn in as the sixth Confederate secretary of war. Had history taken a different course, he might have been sitting in the White House, serving as president over a truly United States. At the age of thirty-six, he had been elected vice president of the United States; four years later the Democratic Party nominated him for president. But the party was badly splintered and Republican Abraham Lincoln won the election. Breckinridge returned to his native Kentucky, where he was quickly elected to the United States Senate. Kentucky stayed in the Union, but his fellow senators suspected him of passing information to the Confederates and even though he had opposed secession, he resigned from the Senate and signed on as a general in the Confederate Army. Now, with the war lost, President Jefferson Davis turned to Breckinridge to run the War Department.

On his first day in office, Breckinridge ordered status reports from his commanders and found them uniformly negative.[1] The South had less than 100,000 effective soldiers, the North nearly one million, and while Northerners now flocked to the Union banner with victory in sight, the Confederate armies were suffering record desertions. On a good day, the South lost only 1,000 soldiers, and they usually took their horses and guns with them. Nearly half of the Confederate Army was absent without leave and the South had never been able to develop an effective method for dealing with deserters. A few soldiers were executed for desertion, but the penalty was unevenly enforced — some courts released deserters entirely — and the South used amnesty to lure deserters back into the ranks.[2]

Northern armies had shut down Confederate factories and it was becoming increasingly difficult to deliver supplies to the troops that remained.

Breckinridge decided that the South had just one chance: If Lee and his army could turn South and join forces with General Joseph Johnston, the two armies might be able to defeat General William Sherman, then turn North and defeat General U.S. Grant. But the plan had been considered before and rejected. On February 23, Lee told Davis, "The idea is good, but the means are lacking."[3] There would be no union of the two Confederate armies.

Now, there was little for Breckinridge to do; all of his armies from Mobile to Richmond were on the defensive, so there was no grand strategy to design. Grant and Sherman would determine where the Confederate armies went, not he. He knew there was no chance for military victory and turned his attention to the welfare of the soldiers who continued to fight. He complained to Davis that the Confederate dollar had lost so much value that a soldier's monthly pay could not even buy a pair of socks, and Breckinridge knew that planting season was coming and surrendering soldiers would be stranded hundreds of miles from their homes with no money for food or travel.[4]

By March, the pace at the capital had slackened. The Confederate Congress left town after passing a few final bills and resolutions. In a backhanded slap at Davis, the Congress passed a bill calling for the appointment of a general-in-chief. The officer would be the "ranking officer of the Army." Obviously, the Congress had Lee in mind for the post, and it was their way of telling Davis they did not like his handling of the war. On February 6, Lee was named commander-in-chief, but he had his hands full worrying about the Army of Northern Virginia and could not pause to worry about the other armies.[5]

The Congress also passed a bill approving the use of slaves as soldiers in the Confederate Army. But it was another useless gesture. Throughout the war, blacks had helped the Confederacy by working on the farms while their masters went off to war, and slaves were used in some trades to free the whites for battle. But 200,000 blacks had served in the Union Army and Abraham Lincoln said that the black soldiers had been decisive in bringing victory to the Union.[6] Throughout the war, plans for using slaves to fight for the South had come and gone. At the beginning of the war, the Confederate government rejected the idea, claiming that there were plenty of white volunteers to fight. Even after the Confederate defeat at Gettysburg, Davis maintained that the slaves were not needed.[7] The slave owners were reluctant to surrender their property; the slave might be wounded or killed in battle, making the investment worthless. On November 7, 1864, Davis finally asked for permission to use slaves as soldiers and on March 16, 1865, Congress gave its approval.[8]

The Congress also approved a resolution blaming most

of the South's failures on Davis, then left town quickly as the sound of Grant's cannons became louder and even the windows of the capitol rattled. On their way out of town, they could see a handful of black soldiers marching in Confederate uniforms in the center of Richmond.

On March 30, the rain was heavy around Richmond and Petersburg, turning the roads to mud and making movement impossible. For Lee's army, the rain was welcome, it bogged down the Union armies on the Petersburg front where General Phil Sheridan was waiting to attack Lee's right flank. But it was only a temporary reprieve, and by Friday morning, March 31, the skies had cleared around Petersburg, Sheridan made his move toward Dinwiddie Court House, but Confederate General George Pickett managed to turn Sheridan back, if only temporarily. Pickett knew that he could not hold Sheridan's men again, and began pulling back toward Five Forks.

Fannie Walker, a clerk in the War Department, was leaving work with a group of friends, when her chief clerk, Dr. Cooke, asked her to stay and copy a few more letters. She agreed and scanned the first letter, her eyes moving quickly to the bottom where she spotted the signature, "R. E. Lee." She quickly turned to Cooke and said, "Oh, Doctor, if this is true, we are lost." Cooke looked at the letter from Lee and immediately spotted the key line, "We cannot hold Petersburg." Cooke turned to the girl, put his finger to his lips and said, "Remember, mum's the word."[9]

A copy of the message was quickly delivered to Davis, who now knew that Richmond was in danger of falling. Davis decided that it was too soon to move his government, but his family was another matter. Already, he had sent William J. Bromwell, the chief clerk of the State Department to Danville with important Confederate papers.[10]

Davis left his office immediately and walked the short

4

distance to his home at Clay and 12th streets as a light rain fell. His wife Varina met him at the door and could tell that something was wrong, his face was ashen and his walk was stiff, almost mechanical, and as she took hold of his arm, she saw for the first time that he was shaking.[11]

Mrs. Davis wrote, "He said for the future his headquarters must be in the field, and that our presence would only embarrass and grieve, instead of comforting him." But Mrs. Davis did not want to go. "Very averse to flight, and unwilling at all times to leave him, I argued the question with him and pleaded to be permitted to remain...."

But Davis quickly stopped her arguments. She listened quietly as Davis told her, "I have confidence in your capacity to take care of our babies, and understand your desire to assist and comfort me, but you can do this in but one way, and that is by going yourself and taking our children to a place of safety."

She hesitated, and he assured her they would be together when the war was over. But in an emotional voice he added, "If I live you can come to me when the struggle is ended, but I do not expect to survive the destruction of constitutional liberty."

Mrs. Davis began packing immediately, starting with the silverware. But Davis stopped her, saying there would not be room. She suggested that it be left with their friends in Richmond, but Davis warned against it. "They may be exposed to inconvenience or outrage by their effort to serve us," Davis said.

She put the silver down and went to the kitchen, where there were several barrels of flour she had purchased and told Davis she wanted to take them with her. "You cannot remove anything in the shape of food from here, the people want it, and you must leave it here." She then turned to her husband and asked if she could take her bric-a-brac, small personal items her husband had dismissed as trumpery in the past. Davis said no, there would not be enough space. They decided that the best course of action would be to take the silver and bric-a-brac to one of the scores of auction houses and sell it to the highest bidder.

Davis sent a telegram to Charlotte, North Carolina, to arrange for a house for his wife and the small group that would accompany her.

The packing was finished and Mrs. Davis would take only some clothes for herself and her four young children, Maggie, nine; Jefferson, Jr., seven; Willie, four, and the baby, Varina Anne, nine months. Mrs. Davis had lost another child in infancy, and in 1864, her son Joe had been killed when he fell from the balcony of their house while playing.

It was time to leave, but there was one piece of un-finished business. Davis brought out a pistol and showed her how to use it. "You can at least, if reduced to the last extremity, force your assailants to kill you, but I charge you solemnly to leave when you hear the enemy are approaching; and if you cannot remain undisturbed in our own country, make for the Florida coast and take a ship there for a foreign country."

Before they left, a messenger arrived from the auction house with a check for $28,400 for the goods they had disposed of. It was too late to cash the check and Davis pulled out a small pouch and handed his wife a stack of gold coins, keeping only five dollars for himself.

The rain was coming down harder, a cold rain that made her departure all the more dreary. Davis, his wife and children rode to the station with her sister, Mrs. Maggie Howell; Ellen, a mulatto maid; James Jones, a mulatto coach-man, and Burton Harrison, Davis' personal secretary and a relative of his first wife. At the Richmond & Danville Station, they were joined by Midshipman James Morris Morgan, who would act as the guard for Mrs. Davis. It was not an unpleasant duty for Morgan, since the daughters of Treasury Secretary George A. Trenholm would be traveling with Mrs. Davis, and Morgan was engaged to Betty Trenholm.

Davis escorted his wife aboard the dilapidated railroad car, the paint was weathered and the once plush seats were soiled and ruined. Arranging a special train was impossible, and Mrs. Davis and her children were taking the regular train to Charlotte. Morgan thought the train must contain fleas. Davis embraced his wife and said goodby.

As Davis turned to go, his daughter Maggie grabbed his leg and hung on. It looked as if Davis might finally break down, but he held his composure. His son Jeff did begin to cry, tearfully begging to remain in Richmond with his father. Davis turned away and walked to the platform and watched as the train pulled out slowly. Mrs. Davis watched her husband and thought he looked as though "he thought he was looking his last upon us."[12]

The train carrying Mrs. Davis traveled just twelve miles before stopping for the night because it was unable to climb a slight grade. No arrangements had been made for sleeping and the women slept in the baggage cars using their coats to protect themselves from the rain that leaked into the cars. They reached Danville the following day, but decided not to stop. They arrived in Charlotte on Tuesday.

In Richmond, the end of the rains Saturday morning brought a beautiful springlike day, the trees beginning to bloom, but few had time to look at them.

Montgomery, Alabama had been the first capital of the Confederacy, the city where Davis was sworn in as provisional president on February 18, 1861. The city had just two hotels and was far too small to satisfy the needs of the Confederate government. The search for a new capital began and Richmond became the political choice. The South needed Virginia in the Confederacy, but the secessionist fever that gripped the other Southern states was not so strong in Virginia. The Western counties were opposed to leaving the Union, and the Virginia Convention approved secession by the relatively close vote of 88 to 55.[13] As a reward for joining the Confederacy, Richmond was selected to be the home of the Confederate government.

Now, it was a dubious honor. Before the war, Richmond had been a prosperous city of 40,000, but when it became the capital, the population nearly doubled overnight as job seekers, officials, gamblers, soldiers and prostitutes descended upon the city. Soon, the hotels were overflowing and tents began appearing around the city. Virginia had taken the brunt of the fighting, giving more of its sons and money than any other state.

As early as 1862, government officials had considered the possibility that Richmond might be captured, and on May 27, 1864, Congress authorized Davis to begin a search for another capital, should evacuation be necessary.[14]

Richmond had become a strange mix of young soldiers missing arms, legs, or even eyes; soldiers preparing to move to the front and soldiers fleeing battle. At Metropolitian Hall, there was a benefit performance to raise money for a Memphis widow whose husband had been killed in battle. On Broad Street, a new play was opening at the Richmond Theater and at the Opera House on Franklin Street, Budd & Buckley's Minstrels with "Their side-splitting jokes" gave a repeat performance of the burlesque on "Recruiting Unbleached Virginians in the Confederate Army."[15]

There were hundreds of hurried marriages between young girls and soldiers moving to the front. The gamblers did boomtown business, but their gains were in Confederate money, now posted at sixty dollars to one dollar in gold. The newspapers were printed on thinner paper each day, they contained hundreds of advertisements for auction sales, mostly for the household goods of the city's once proud homes. Some residents went without food, while black market operators openly sold their goods.

A.R. Tomlinson, who had been wounded in battle, was now a sergeant of the guard at Winder Hospital. He seldom ate, and when he did receive food, it was gruel and small pieces of bread. He could not bring himself to eat the meats the surgeons managed to consume. "The surgeons and matrons ate rats and said they were as good as squirrels, but, having seen the rats in the morgue running over the bodies of dead soldiers, I had no relish for them."[16]

The craze in the city was the Starvation Party, with participants dressing up in their finest prewar clothing, now faded and often torn. No refreshments were permitted and the elegant crystal bowls were filled with water.

But the people in the city were better off than Lee's men in the trenches. General Grant's strategy was simple, stretch the Confederate lines to the breaking point and then send units to probe for the weakest points. In some places, the lines were so thin that one Confederate soldier could barely see the next man on the line. Now, Grant was ready to probe at Five Forks, a crucial Confederate stronghold. Lee told Pickett to "Hold Five Forks at all hazards."[17] If the right flank of the Confederate line at Petersburg should fall, the entire retreat route of the Army of Northern Virginia would be threatened. Pickett's men began digging in, singing *Annie Laurie* and *Dixie*. The attack came late in the afternoon as General Phil Sheridan's cavalry and General Gouverneur Warren's Fifth Corps of infantry attacked at Five Forks. As the dismounted cavalry of Sheridan attacked in front, Warren's corps got on the left flank of the enemy and both forces crushed the defenders. For Sheridan, the victory was more than he could have hoped for. He had encircled Lee's flank on the right and had almost encircled the city of Petersburg. The

Union Army was close to the vital South Side Railroad, and if that fell, the Confederates would be cut off from supplies and a route for escape.

The end was near, and Lee sent two messages that evening, one to Davis, the other to Breckinridge.

> Mr. President:
> The movement of Genl Grant to Dinwiddie Court House seriously threatens our position, and diminishes our ability to maintain our present lines in front of Petersburg. In the first place it cuts us off from our depot at Stony Creek at which point forage for the cavalry was delivered by the Weldon Railroad and upon which we relied to maintain it. It also renders it more difficult to withdraw from our position, cuts us off from the White Oak road, and gives the enemy an advantageous point on our right and rear. From this point I fear he can readily cut both the South Side & Danville Railroads being far superior to us in cavalry. This in my opinion obliged us to prepare for the necessity of evacuating our position on James River at once, and also to consider the best means of accomplishing it, and our future course. I should like very much to have the views of Your Excellency upon this matter as well as counsel, and would repair to Richmond for the purpose, did I not feel that my presence here is necessary. Should I find it practicable, I will do so, but should it be convenient for Your Excellency or the Secretary of War to visit headquarters, I should be glad to see you. The reported advance of [Gen. George] Stoneman from the west, and the movement of the enemy upon the Roanoke, add to our difficulties.
> Very respectfully, your obt serv't
> R. E. Lee
> Genl[18]

To Breckinridge, Lee wrote a more detailed description of the day's military events. Breckinridge knew that Lee would have to abandon his James River position sooner or later, but the message made him angry. Three days earlier, Breckinridge told Lee that he was preparing to move the government stores, "But if possible, would like to know whether we may probably count on a period of ten or twelve days." Lee replied, "I know of no reason to prevent your counting on the time suggested."[19] Now, Lee was telling Breckinridge that instead of more than a week to complete the job, Breckinridge might have just twenty-four hours.

Davis also sent a message to Lee on that Saturday: "The question is often asked 'will we hold Richmond,' to which my only answer is, if we can; it is purely a question of military power. The distrust is increasing, and embarrasses in many ways."[20]

John H. Reagan, the Confederate postmaster general, spent most of Saturday night in the War Department awaiting further word from Lee.

At 4:40 Sunday morning, April 2, Union troops advanced under heavy fog along the Petersburg line. The Confederate defenses all but collapsed. By seven a.m. the drive was fully underway; Horatio Wright's Sixth Corps ran through the Confederates at the South Side Railroad. The Union troops kept pushing forward, surprised at meeting so little opposition. By noon, only two Confederate forts held their ground, Gregg and Baldwin. In the afternoon, the Confederates stiffened, but Lee knew it was only temporary.

Lee now sent the first of what would be many messages to Richmond, a telegram to Breckinridge:

> I see no prospect of doing more than holding our position here till night. I am not certain that I can do that. If I can I shall withdraw tonight North of the Appomattox, and if possible it will be better to withdraw the whole line tonight from James River. The brigades on Hatcher's Run are cut off from us. Enemy

have broken through our lines and intercepted between
us and them, and there is no bridge over which they
can cross the Appomattox this side of Goode's or
Beaver's, which are not very far from the Danville Railroad. Our only chance, then, of concentrating our
forces, is to do so near Danville Railroad, which I shall
endeavor to do at once. I advise that all preparations
be made for leaving Richmond tonight. I will advise
you later, according to circumstances.

R. E. Lee[21]

Reagan was waiting when the message arrived at the
War Department at eight a.m. Reagan dispatched the message
to Breckinridge, then waited with other aides. They paced
the wooden floors without making a sound for nearly ninety
minutes. At 9:30, a second telegram arrived, this one for
Davis:

I think it is absolutely necessary that we should
abandon our position tonight. I have given all the
necessary orders on the subject to the troops, and the
operation, though difficult, I hope will be performed
successfully. I have directed General [Walter] Stevens to
send an officer to Your Excellency to explain the routes
to you by which the troops will be moved to Amelia Court
House, and furnish you with a guide and any assistance
that you may require for yourself.

R. E. Lee[22]

Reagan went looking for Davis to deliver the message
personally. Davis was on his way to church, the imposing St.
Pauls at the corner of Grace and Ninth streets. Reagan later
wrote that he found Davis and General Frank Lubbock on the
street and Davis said he would await another message from
Lee before deciding what to do. Davis said he did not recall
receiving the message from Reagan.[23]

12

Davis went directly to his pew, number 63, and sat down. Navy Secretary Stephen R. Mallory, sitting nearby, said Davis' face, "varied not from that cold, stern sadness which four years of harassing mental labor had stamped upon it ... the cold, calm eyes, the sunken cheek, the compressed lip, were all as impenetrable as an iron mask."[24]

At 10:40, another message came from Lee, this one to Breckinridge.

> It is absolutely necessary that we should abandon our position tonight, or run the risk of being cut off in the morning. I have given all the orders to officers on both sides of the river, & have taken every precaution that I can to make the movement successful. It will be a difficult operation, but I hope not impracticable. Please give all orders that you find necessary in & about Richmond. The troops will all be directed to Amelia Court House.
>
> R. E. Lee[25]

A clerk was dispatched from the War Department to alert Davis. It was nearly noon when the young civilian clerk entered the church and approached church sexton William Irving and whispered, "I must see President Davis." Irving replied, "I'll call him when the prayer's done."

The youth waited a moment, pacing in the church foyer, then said, "I cannot wait any longer." He scribbled a message for Davis: "General Lee telegraphs that he can hold his position no longer. Come to the office immediately. Breckinridge." Irving read the note and quietly walked to Davis, who glanced at it and left the church.[26]

As the President walked from the church, Irving went down the aisle, tapping key administration figures on the shoulder. General Josiah Gorgas, head of the Ordnance Department, left quickly and was followed by his aide, Colonel

William Groun. The minister, Dr. Charles Minnigerode, continued with his sermon, but he was clearly distracted as more than a dozen men left the church.

Davis walked alone down Ninth Street to Capitol Square, then up the hill to the Treasury Building. The fate of the city was still a well-kept secret and he passed a number of people out for a walk. Mallory described it as "a clear, beautiful day in Richmond.... The temperature wooed the people abroad, a pleasant air swept the foliage and flowers of the Capitol grounds, the sun beamed upon its bronze group of conscript fathers ... and the church bells pealed their invitations.... The old city had never, during the war, worn an aspect more serene and quiet; and yet at that very moment the hours of the Confederacy ... were being numbered."[27]

Davis found the clerks and aides working their way through a mountain of documents, deciding which should be removed from Richmond, which should be burned and which should be left behind. He dispatched clerks to round up the Cabinet members for an emergency meeting in a third-floor room of what had been the U.S. Customs house before the war. The Cabinet members quietly took their seats, except for Attorney General George Davis, who had attended a different church that morning and could not be located, and Treasury Secretary George Trenholm, who was suffering from neuralgia and was confined to his bed.

Jefferson Davis briefly outlined plans for the evacuation, each department head would be responsible for supervising the packing of his records and have them delivered to the Richmond & Danville Depot that evening. There would be eight trains leaving Richmond for Danville and the message was clear, anything or anyone not on one of those trains would remain behind in Richmond. The sound of a new round of Union cannon fire shortened the meeting and the members hurried back to their offices.

14

The Confederates Leave

The President returned to his official residence to supervise the packing of his personal possessions. He found four of his Negro servants drunk and the others were in a surly temper. In the excitement of the past two days, he had forgotten to cash the auction house check for $28,500 and now gave it to John Hendera, the Confederate treasurer, and said, "Have it cashed at the Bank of Richmond, if you can." The money was important to Davis now, the income from his giant Mississippi cotton empire had long since stopped and the Friday trip to the auction house was not the first one for Davis. He had already sold his horses, even the matched team of carriage horses used by his wife. Some friends found out about the sale and purchased the horses to return to Davis. In stores around Richmond, there were a number of possessions once cherished by Davis and his wife. In one store window was a green silk gown once worn proudly by Mrs. Davis, in another shop her laces and silk gloves.

Inflation was hurting Davis along with everyone else. A pound of bacon cost twenty dollars, live hens were fifty and butter was twenty dollars a pound. And now, as rumors that the city was about to fall began to spread, the value of the Confederate dollar fell even more. Hendera returned from the Bank of Richmond with the news that the bank would not honor the check of the President of the Confederacy. Davis said, "Take it along, perhaps we can cash it in Danville, or along the route." The only money Davis had was the five dollars in gold coins.

Davis gave detailed instructions to the servants, he wanted the marble bust of himself crated and given to his friend John Davis, who promised, "I'll put it where no Yankee will ever find it."[28]

The servant left with the bust and Davis started giving orders to Mrs. Omelia, the housekeeper. He told her to make sure his daughter Maggie's saddle was taken aboard the train,

15

but he could not decide what to do with his paintings. He was constantly interrupted by aides bringing him messages.

One of the messages came from Lee. Even though he was obviously preoccupied with the plans for evacuating his army, Lee paused in midafternoon to respond to a letter Davis had sent him the day before dealing with efforts to recruit Negro soldiers.

> Mr. President:
>
> Your letter of the 1st is just received. I have been willing to detach officers to recruit Negro troops, and have sent in the names of many who are desirous of recruiting companies, battalions, or regiments to the War Department. After receiving the General Orders on that subject, establishing recruiting depots in the several States, I supposed that his mode of raising the troops was preferred. I will continue to submit the names of those who offer for the service, and whom I deem competent, to the War Department; but among the numerous applications which are presented, it is difficult for me to decide who are suitable for the duty. I am glad Your Excellency has made an appeal to the Governors of the States, and hope it will have a good effect. I have had a great desire to confer with you upon our condition, and would have been to Richmond before this; but anticipating movements of the enemy, which have occurred, I felt unwilling to be absent. I have considered our position very critical, but have hoped that the enemy might expose himself in some way that we might take advantage of, and cripple him.
>
> Knowing when Sheridan moved on our right that our cavalry would be unable to resist successfully his advance upon our communications, I detached Pickett's division to support it. At first Pickett succeeded in driving the enemy, who fought stubbornly, and after being reinforced by the 5th Corps (U.S.), obliged Pickett to recede to the Five Forks on the

Dinwiddie Court House and Ford's road, where unfortunately he was yesterday defeated. To relieve him, I had to again draw out three brigades under Genl Anderson, which so weakened our front line that the enemy last night and this morning succeeded in penetrating it near the Church road, separating our troops around the town from those on Hatcher's Run. This has enabled him to extend to the Appomattox, thus enclosing and obliging us to contract our lines to the city. I have directed the troops from the lines on Hatcher's Run, thus severed from us, to fall back towards Amelia Court House, and I do not see how I can possibly help withdrawing from the city to the north side of the Appomattox tonight. There is no bridge over the Appomattox above the point nearer than Goode's and Bevill's over which the troops above mentioned could cross to the north side and be made available to us. Otherwise I might hold this position for a day or two longer; but would have to evacuate it eventually, and I think it better for us to abandon the whole line of James River tonight if practicable. I have sent preparatory orders to all the officers, and will be able to tell by night whether or not we can remain here another day, but I think every hour now adds to our difficulties. I regret to be obliged to write such a hurried letter to Your Excellency, but I am in the presence of the enemy endeavoring to resist his advance.

I am most respectfully & truly yrs
R. E. Lee[29]

At some point during the afternoon, Davis sent a message to Lee, apparently to make sure that Lee would be forced to leave his lines. Lee telegraphed:

YOUR TELEGRAM RECEIVED. I THINK IT WILL BE NECESSARY TO MOVE TONIGHT. I SHALL CAMP THE TROOPS HERE NORTH OF THE APPOMATTOX. THE ENEMY IS SO STRONG THAT THEY WILL CROSS ABOVE

James Grant, a wealthy friend of Davis' stopped by to carry off some items to his farm in the country for safekeeping. "Take Mrs. Davis' carriage with you," Davis urged him but Grant only shook his head and said, "I don't believe I'd risk that, sir."

"Well, then take it to the depot, I'll carry it along," Davis said. Time was growing short and he shouted to no one in particular, "Save the inkstand."[31]

Finally, everything was done, the big house was nearly empty and there was nothing for Davis to do but sit and wait for the train that would take him out of Richmond.

At the Treasury Department, Walter Philbrook, the senior teller, supervised the packing of what remained of the Confederate treasury. There were some gold nuggets, silver bricks, Mexican silver coins and gold double eagles. In all, it was worth perhaps $500,000, and nearly half belonged to the Richmond banks.

When the war began, the Confederacy sold $15 million in bonds, backing it with the South's most valuable commodity, cotton. The money went quickly, and in August 1861, the Confederate government approved a war tax on property. But collecting the tax proved to be a problem the South could not overcome. First, most people expected the war to last only a few months and be relatively inexpensive. And the South had no machinery for collecting the tax and as a result it was often administered unfairly. As the war dragged on, the South tried other means to finance the fighting — a tax on produce in 1863 and a law to devalue treasury notes are the most notable; all ended in failure. By April 1865, the Confederacy was $700 million in debt and overall inflation was nearly 6,000 percent.

18

Treasury Clerk Philbrook was concerned about the safety of the money and asked for protection. Sixty cadets from the Confederate Naval Academy were recruited under the command of Captain William Parker and told by Navy Secretary Mallory, "You will go with the President and Cabinet to guard the gold treasure." He said they were "chosen for dangerous service, because you are brave, honest and discreet and gentlemen."[32]

Parker was unsure how long his mission would last, and ordered the company cook to prepare only three days of rations. He and his men were ordered to report to the train station at six o'clock that evening. Micajah Clark, the chief clerk of the executive office, packed Davis' papers and took them to the depot. The treasury clerks took the gold to the depot, where it was loaded onto a freight car under the supervision of the midshipmen. Since half of the treasure belonged to the Richmond banks, they wanted to keep a close eye on their money. The banks each assigned a junior officer to travel with the treasure. The bank clerks, who had been roused from their homes to perform this unwanted duty, were concerned about leaving their wives in a city that was about to fall, and they decided to bring them along. Now, the midshipmen, the bank clerks and their wives waited at the depot with their gold.

At four p.m., Richmond Mayor Joseph Mayo called a meeting of the city council to advise it that the Confederate government was about to evacuate the city. It hardly came as news to the council members. Mayo announced that all liquor would be destroyed. Protection of the city would be left in the hands of the home guard, a collection of wounded soldiers, old men and government workers whose worth was questionable. They could not be counted on in what would be their one moment of action.

At dusk, Davis carefully combed his hair and beard

and put on his wide-brimmed felt hat, his Confederate-grey waistcoat and Prince Albert coat. After four years of hectic activity, the house was strangely quiet now. As darkness descended on the city, Davis left the house with his secretary, John Taylor Wood, and two aides, Colonel William Johnston of Kentucky and Governor Francis Lubbock of Texas. Wood carried Davis' suitcase, which contained coats, trousers, waistcoats, linen skirts, a silk tie, a dressing robe, a roll of corn-plaster, and a pair of leggings, some underclothing, extra shoelaces, a small dressing case, a razor strap, a comb, brush, two towels, two cigars, a nine-shooter pistol, a double-barreled revolver, two holster pistols, a pistol case, some ammunition and pictures of his wife, General Lee and himself.

As he left the house, he told his housekeeper, Mrs. Omelia, to give the house a good cleaning, since he had no way of knowing who would occupy it the next day, and wanted to make a good impression on the Union officers.[32]

At the station, Davis found mass confusion. He and his aides had to push their way through the crowds to reach the train. No one was really in charge. Throughout the day, there had been a series of conflicting orders. First, "Send all trains to Richmond," then later, "Hold all trains at Danville."[33] The train carrying Davis had been scheduled to leave at eight p.m., but Davis had some last minute business to conduct and he stood on the platform talking with aides and signing papers while people surged around him. Some were trying to buy their way onto the train, while those with passes squeezed into boxcars.

One of Davis' servants, Robert, tugged at the President's sleeve and said, "Miss Omelia won't let me pack the stuff, and they ain't much here. She even took the groceries out of the chest. I can't find Miss Maggie's saddle nowhere." Davis was still concerned about his wife's carriage and ordered the trainmen to put it aboard the train. But they

20

argued that there was not enough room on top of the cars. "Put it on the next train," Davis said, and was told it would be done.

As the soldiers called for the passengers to board the train, Davis found that there was more for him to do. Another servant, Tippy, had been left behind at the President's house and another servant, Spencer, had come despite Davis' order that he remain in Richmond. A slave shouted over the crowd to Davis, "They left the spoons and forks, sir." Davis sent another servant, Bradford, back to the mansion to find his wife's possessions and told him to leave the city the following day with Breckinridge.[34]

Breckinridge had decided not to accompany Davis, but to remain in Richmond so he could join Lee on the front the following day. In Petersburg, Lee fought to keep his lines intact to allow Davis and the Cabinet time to escape. Finally, he turned to an aide and said, "This is sad business, colonel. It has happened as I told them in Richmond it would happen. The line has been stretched until it is broken."[35]

By ten p.m., the train was loaded and everyone except Davis was ready to leave. Davis was hoping that he would receive further word from Lee—perhaps that the tide had turned and the evacuation would not be necessary. But finally, about eleven, he ordered the train to leave.[36]

When Davis and the Confederate government arrived in Richmond four years earlier, they found a prosperous city. Now, as they left, it was a city without civilization. Even before the train left, the shutters in the finer homes were closed and the lights turned down. The city streets were becoming rowdier as the crowds of flashily dressed hangers-on at the hotels and saloons emerged looking for plunder.

Fleeing city officials had ordered government storehouses burned, but the fires quickly spread. Most of the Ordnance Department officials, led by General Josiah Gorgas, the chief of the ordnance, left on a separate train at the same time as Davis, but some were unable to get onto the train. Ordnance Department Chief Clerk Joseph Haw, one of those unable to reach the train, watched as the city burned. "The storehouses were wide open and filled with men, women and children, both black and white. For light, they were burning bits of paper and dropping them on the floor still burning. One man fell through an elevator hatch and nobody bothered themselves about him, so bent were they on destruction."

Elizabeth Saunders looked from her window and saw "People were running about everywhere with plunder and provisions. Barrels and boxes were rolled and tumbled about the streets. Military authorities decided that it would be best to destroy the liquor before the mobs could get to it. They broke the kegs open and dumped the whiskey into the gutters, but it did not stop the crowds who rushed to scoop it up with pitchers, cups or their hands from the gutters."

The night air was filled with yells, curses, cries of distress and laughter. E.T. Watehall, a fourteen-year-old lad, recalled that he went looking for food during the night, stopping by Antoni's Confectionery and found men in Confederate uniforms smashing the door in. One of the employees screamed, "Take all you want, but don't ruin us." A nearby jewelry store window was broken and the counters had been rifled by the crowd. In order to find their way, they lit pieces of paper and torches, the sparks flew off and started fires around the city.

Haw and his ordnance men returned to the depot hours later and were able to jam into a freight car, sitting on top of pig lead and bullet molds. The car also contained mattresses and household furniture belonging to fleeing Confederate officials. As the train moved, Haw heard sounds from the top of the train and wondered who was on top. He soon realized that wounded soldiers had been placed on top of the cars.[37]

As dawn came, the city was a smoking ruin, the destruction the residents had feared from the Union armies had been done by the Confederates. General Kemper, who was wounded in Pickett's charge at Gettysburg, was commanding the local defense units, but could find no one to give him orders.[38] By early morning, the last Confederate troops had left the city. Behind them, the city was awakening to survey the damage.

Richmond Mayor Mayo, the eighty-year-old man who had vowed in 1862 that he would never surrender the city, now rode out with two other men in a rickety carriage to meet the Union troops. As he approached the troops he asked for a white flag. Neither had a white flag, so they retired to a nearby tree and tore the tail from one of their white shirts and attached it to a stick.[39]

At eight a.m., the Union cavalry entered the city, their horses pounding through the city streets heading directly for the Capitol. They hardly noticed the men and women who were sleeping in the city square with their remaining possessions. The infantry came close behind as the Union band played *The Girl I Left Behind*. Then came the Negro Union troops, playing *Dixie*, and at 8:15 the Union flag was raised over Richmond. By evening, the city was quiet.

II. Aboard the Last Train

The train carrying Davis and his Cabinet moved slowly through Virginia, following the only route of escape still open, southwest to Burkeville, then South to Danville. The railroads of the South had lagged behind those of the North even before the war, and four years of fighting had reduced the Southern rails to a decaying disaster. In 1861, there had been talk of putting the railroads under government control, but the idea was quickly dismissed by the forces who found national control of private enterprise to be repugnant.

In late February 1865, with time running out, the Confederate Congress acted, placing the rails in government hands, but it was too late, the rail system was too far gone to be of any use.[40] Now Davis was seeing firsthand the condition of the rails: the 140-mile trip to Danville should have taken four hours, but the train crawled along at barely nine miles an hour, pulled by the engine "Charles Sedden." The trip took sixteen hours.

The men in the train wore two faces. Inside the train they sat quietly, fearing Union patrols in the area would swoop down and capture them. But as the train passed groups of citizens who had turned out to wave to their leaders, Davis would put on a brave expression and wave. Lt. John S. Wise, the son of one of Lee's aides, who was stationed at Clover Station, some eighty miles from Richmond, said the first evacuation trains began to pass him about midnight, stopping for water and wood. The passengers from the first trains were upbeat as they stopped. The army's not beaten or demoralized, one passenger said. Other passengers said the Army was retreating in good order; they predicted that Lee would quickly turn the tables now that he no longer had the long lines around Richmond to defend. There was no reason to be concerned.

Wise was encouraged until the Davis train came through about three a.m. and he saw the president. Sitting beside the window, Davis smiled to the cheers of the small crowd but, Wise said, "his expression showed physical and mental exhaustion."[41]

Mallory later wrote, "the train moved in gloomy silence over the James River. A commanding view of the river front of the city was thus afforded, and as the fugitives receded from its flickering lights, many and sad were the commentaries they made upon the Confederate cause."[42]

Jefferson Davis sat next to General Braxton Bragg; nearby was the President's physician, Dr. Garnett. Postmaster General Reagan sat whittling a stick, never quite achieving the sharp point he wanted. He continued to whittle until there was almost nothing left of the stick. Treasury Secretary Trenholm was seriously ill and lay across one of the train seats; his wife, the only woman in the car, sat nearby. Mrs. Breckinridge had remained behind in Richmond, Mrs. Mallory was already in Georgia, Reagan and Attorney

General George Davis were widowers, and Secretary of State Judah P. Benjamin had been separated from his wife for years.

Wise called it a "government on wheels. It was the marvelous and incongruous debris of the wreck of the Confederate capital. There were very few women on these trains, but among the last in the long procession were trains bearing indiscriminate cargoes of men and things. In one car was a cage with an African parrot and a box of tame squirrels and a hunchback."[43]

To help Trenholm cope with his illness, two hampers of peach brandy had been brought aboard, but Benjamin quickly found nonmedical uses for it. Navy Secretary Mallory sampled the brandy and wrote, "Our fugitives recovered their spirits."[44]

The final Cabinet member present was George Davis, who sat quietly by himself. Also in the Davis car were Lewis E. Harvie, the president of the Richmond & Danville Railroad, and Dr. Moses Hoge, a Presbyterian minister in Richmond who had been advised to leave Richmond because of his strong anti-Union views.

George Davis, a North Carolinian, had been a strong backer of the Confederacy, serving in the Provisional Congress at Montgomery and as a Confederate senator in Richmond. He lost a race for reelection and returned home to Wilmington to practice law. North Carolina Governor Zebulon Vance had become a leading critic of the Davis Administration and in 1864 it appeared that he might work to bring the State back into the Union. Jefferson Davis thought that by giving a North Carolinian a Cabinet post he could quiet the storm of protest. At the age of forty-four, George Davis got the job as attorney general.

The Confederate Constitution called for a Justice Department, headed by an attorney general, and a federal court system. But no court system was ever established, and Davis did little besides offer legal opinions to the President and other Cabinet members. He had nevertheless become a close friend of the President, who sought his advice on a wide range of issues.

John Reagan, the Tennessee farm boy who made his reputation in Texas, was the Cabinet member closest to Davis personally. Reagan had moved to Texas in 1839 at the age of twenty-one; he fought Indians, surveyed, farmed and practiced law. He served two terms in Congress before the Civil War began. He considered himself a moderate but in the Texas convention he supported leaving the Union. Reluctantly, he agreed to serve as postmaster general, but as the war dragged on, his duties shrank. The United States had established a well-organized postal system in the South seventy years earlier, and even after the Southern states left the Union, the postal system continued to deliver the mail. Federal authorities reasoned that the war would last only a short time and saw no reason to dismantle a complex system only to have to reestablish it in a few months. When the Union finally stopped delivering the mail, Reagan merely extended the existing contracts with the mail carriers and railroads and continued the service.

As the Union armies conquered additional Confederate territory, delivering the mail became more difficult. In 1862, Reagan, stung by criticism, tried to resign, but Davis refused to accept the resignation. Reagan did what no United States postmaster general has managed to do — he made a profit on delivering the mail.

Mallory wrote that Reagan sat "silent and sombre, his eyes as bright and glistening as beads, but evidently seeing nothing around them...."[45]

While Reagan was closest to Davis personally, Secretary of State Judah P. Benjamin was his most trusted political advisor. Benjamin, fifty-three years old, had entered

28

Yale University at the age of fourteen but left under a cloud before graduating. He had served with Davis in the United States Senate, where he distinguished himself as a legal scholar, and twice turned down a seat on the United States Supreme Court. When the war began, Benjamin was named attorney general but as George Davis would later learn, it was a hollow position. He had a small office, largely bare of furniture. It was a frustrating position for the ambitious Benjamin, as he saw the war unfolding and found himself largely on the sidelines. At rare intervals, he was asked for a legal ruling, but he generally spent his time looking for things to do.

Davis and Benjamin had started with a strained relationship but soon became fast friends. When the war was only a few months old, it became clear that Secretary of War Leroy Walker could not handle the job. His lack of qualifications became obvious even before the fighting began, and in September Benjamin was named to take Walker's place. But Benjamin did little better in the job than Walker and quickly became the scapegoat for Army failures.

In February, 1862, the Confederate Congress launched an investigation into the conduct of the war and the following month Davis removed Benjamin as war secretary and named him secretary of state, the third in just one year, following Robert A. Toombs, one of the organizers of the Confederacy who had lusted after the presidency, and Robert M.T. Hunter, another unsuccessful candidate for president. Toombs had been a miserable failure as secretary of state, lacking anything approaching a diplomatic personality. Hunter did even worse and within weeks after he took office he and Davis were quarreling.

The sole responsibility of the secretary of state was to get a foreign nation — any foreign nation — to recognize the Confederacy and offer aid. In the heady days before the fighting began, it had generally been assumed in the South that England would be a natural ally, if not for the love of the new nation then certainly for its need of the cotton produced by the South. France would also be a natural ally because if Napoleon helped the South now, then the South would back his attempts to control Mexico.

But in England, Queen Victoria hesitated; her advisors told her that if the goal was to see the United States damaged, a long war would do that without British intervention. And would it not be wiser to show Her Majesty's British subjects that democracy breeds revolution? In short, why should the British run any risks when the Americans seemed to be doing quite a good job of destroying the United States.

Confederate leaders also figured that the British milling industry would become desperate for Confederate cotton and force England to come to aid the Confederate cause. But when the war began, the British warehouses were overstocked with cotton and the war served to drive up the prices, making the mill owners richer. The cotton shortage did cause unemployment to rise slightly, but being jobless and fighting in a war were hardly the kinds of alternatives which would have the workers marching in the streets demanding a war.

So, Benjamin had served as secretary of state for more than three years, suffering the false hopes and crushing defeats and managed to remain Davis' top advisor. He could later take some comfort from the fact that Napoleon's plan backfired badly. The Emperor stayed out of the Civil War, hoping that the United States would stay out of Mexico, but he was wrong, and when the United States finished with the Confederacy, it turned to pushing the French out of Mexico.

As attorney general, Benjamin presided over an invisible judicial system; as secretary of war, he had failed to distinguish himself and as secretary of state he was unable to gain the recognition of a single nation. And yet as the train headed South, he joked with his fellow passengers. Nearly twenty years after the war, Jefferson Davis would remember Benjamin as "A master of law and the most accomplished statesman I have ever known.[46]

Stephen R. Mallory was one of the original six members of the Davis Cabinet, serving as secretary of the navy throughout the war. Mallory was chosen for the Cabinet as part of Davis' plan to bring geographic balance to the Confederate leadership. Each Cabinet member was from a different state, and certainly Florida was entitled to representation.

Mallory was born in Trinidad, where his father was working on an engineering project, and grew up in Key West, where his widowed mother ran a boarding house. He was elected to the United States Senate from Florida and earned a reputation as an expert on naval affairs; because of that knowledge, he was picked by Davis for the cabinet post. He was hardly the unanimous choice, two delegates from his own state voted against him at the Provisional Congress. In truth, no one was really sure whether Mallory actually supported the Confederacy. He had attended school in the North as a boy and had refused to take part in any efforts toward secession. Mallory would later claim that he had made serious attempts to avoid service in the Confederate Cabinet and had frequently submitted his resignation to Davis, only to have it rejected.[47]

When Mallory took over as navy secretary, he found he had a small office, a desk and almost no sailors. The South, unlike the North, did not have a tradition of seafaring men, and in 1861, when a navy of 2,000 men was authorized, there were not enough volunteers. Congress provided that anyone drafted into the Army could choose the navy, but still not

31

enough men came forward. Finally, in desperation, the courts began offering convicted criminals a choice, prison or joining the Confederate navy.[48] Mallory opened a Naval Academy, but the students never progressed much beyond the training stage, spending much of the war on the training ship Patrick Henry near Richmond.

Mallory realized that there was no way he could compete with the Union navy on anything approaching an even basis, so he turned to unusual weapons in an effort to break the Union blockade of Southern ports and disrupt Union commerce. Mallory placed torpedoes in Southern harbors, a weapon which destroyed more Union ships than all of the sea battles combined — thirty-seven — and he saw the possibilities for ironclad ships and soon had the *Merrimac* fitted with iron plate, renaming it the *Virginia*.

But the leadership of the Confederacy, from Davis down, placed almost total emphasis on the Army, all but ignoring the navy. That may explain why Mallory served as navy secretary for the entire war, while Davis went through six secretaries of war. Mallory would live to see his ideas for ironclad ships spread throughout the world, and torpedoes used by every major nation, but he was never able to break the stranglehold of the Union blockade. He watched helplessly as the Confederacy slowly starved for war materials while valuable cotton rotted on Southern docks.

The final Cabinet member on the train was Treasury Secretary George Trenholm, perhaps the wealthiest man in the South at the beginning of the war. His wealth included steamships, railroads, hotels, cotton, real estate, plantations and thousands of slaves. Trenholm was a strong supporter of the Confederacy, but the cause also increased his fortune. Josiah Gorgas estimated that by 1863, Trenholm had made nine million dollars in blockade running.

Trenholm had been named treasury secretary in July

1864 and had spent the next nine months trying with little success to find some way to stop the financial havoc. But there was little he could do to save the Confederacy from insolvency.

Mallory wrote that Trenholm had "a never give up the ship sort of air," and "referred to other great national causes which had been redeemed from far gloomier reverses than ours."[49]

III. In Danville Davis Waits for Lee

As the train moved through Virginia on Monday morning, April 3, 1865, Lee's troops moved west with Grant following along a parallel route. Grant no longer feared Lee's army and sought only to keep him from heading South to meet Johnston. Breckinridge joined Lee on Monday morning and the following day wrote Jefferson Davis in Danville.

> I left General Lee at Farmville yesterday morning where he was passing the main body across the river for temporary relief. He will still try to move around toward North Carolina. There was very little firing yesterday and I hear none today. No definite information as to movements of enemy from Junction to Danville. Stoneman's advance reported yesterday to be near Liberty. [Major General Lunsford] Lomax reports enemy in considerable force advancing up Shenandoah Valley. No news from [Gen. John] Echols, but he is supposed to be close to Stoneman's rear. General Lee has sent orders to Lomax to unite with Echols against Stoneman and

35

to [General Raleigh E.] Colston to make firm defense at Lynchburg.

The message ended, "The straggling has been great and the situation was not favorable."[50] Riding on horseback, Breckinridge began his ride to Danville to rejoin Davis.

Although the smoke was still rising from the ashes of Richmond, the small town of Danville was flattered at the arrival of Davis and his Cabinet. Before the war, Danville had opposed joining the Confederacy, agreeing to support the cause only after shots were fired at Fort Sumter. During the war, Danville was a center for holding Union prisoners. The town of 6,000 housed as many as 7,500 prisoners, but only 3,000 survived the war.

As soon as residents learned that the Confederate officials were heading toward Danville, a mass meeting was held at the town hall to make plans for receiving the officials. Danville's *Weekly Register* speculated that Danville would be the new permanent capital of the Confederacy, and residents dreamed of their town being transformed into a great city. When Davis arrived, the railroad depot was jammed with prominent citizens who listened as Davis promised that the struggle would continue. The crowd applauded as the officials left the train. George Davis, the tallest Cabinet member, had to bend down as he left the car to keep from bumping his head. Jefferson Davis told the crowd that the struggle would continue. "I will never consent to abandon to the enemy one foot of the soil of any of the States of the Confederacy."

The President was weary from the trip, but immediately set out to inspect the fortifications of Danville. The fortifications had been erected four years earlier and since then the city had not been threatened. Accompanied by the post commander, Robert E. Withers, Davis viewed the intrenchments and wrote in his memoirs that he found them "as faulty in location as in construction. I promptly proceeded to correct the one and improve the other."[51] In 1861, before he was named President, Davis had envisioned a field command, directing the Confederate armies as he had once directed the war department for the Union. Now, he was not only president, but also military commander of Danville, supervising troops that did not exist to do battle against an enemy that would never come.

From his tour of the defenses, Davis went to the home of Major W.T. Sutherlin on Union Street. Secretary and Mrs. Trenholm, Lubbock and Mallory also stayed at the large Sutherlin home, built with the fortune he had made in tobacco before the war. Benjamin found himself without a place to sleep, but the Rev. Hoge invited him to stay with him at the home of John M. Johnston, cashier at the Bank of Danville.

Some other government officials stayed at the Benedict House on Wilson Street. The town's hotels, the Exchange and Tunstall House, were filled by clerks.

Monday evening, Davis wrote a letter to his wife: "I am unwilling to leave Virginia."[52] In his memoirs, Davis wrote, "The design, as previously arranged with General Lee, was that if he should be compelled to evacuate Petersburg, he would proceed to Danville, make a new defensive line of the Dan and Roanoke rivers and make a combined attack (with Johnston) upon Sherman." If that failed, Davis wrote, "It was expected that reviving hope would bring reinforcements to the army, and Grant being then far removed from his base of supplies, and in the midst of a hostile population, it was thought we might return, drive him from the soil of Virginia, and restore to the people a government deriving its authority from their consent."[53]

Tuesday morning, Davis awoke to find there was no word from Lee, despite anxious inquiries. Most of the telegraph lines around Danville had been cut, severely limiting communication. Admiral Raphael Semmes and 400 crewmen from the scuttled James River flotilla arrived in the morning and Semmes was immediately commissioned a brigadier general and his crewmen changed into an artillery brigade. Semmes was given the job of directing the Danville defenses and scouring the countryside for food and supplies for Lee's army.

Davis called the Cabinet members together at the Sutherlin home. He and Benjamin moved to the home's library to write a proclamation to the people of the Confederacy. Actually, Benjamin did most of the writing, with Davis adding only an occasional phrase or making a suggestion. About noon, Benjamin took the proclamation to the office of the *Weekly Register* and handed the document to Editor Abner Anderson. Benjamin told Anderson, "There are some erasures and interlineations in this. Let me have some paper and I will write a clear copy for your printer."[54] Anderson printed the proclamation as a broadsheet and also as an extra edition of the newspaper.

> It would be unwise, even if it were possible, to conceal the great moral as well as material injury to our cause that must result from the occupation of Richmond by the enemy. It is equally unwise and unworthy to us, as patriots engaged in a most sacred cause, to allow our energies to falter, our spirits to grow faint or our efforts to become relaxed under reverses, however calamitous ... it is for us, my countrymen, to show by our bearing under reverses how wretched has been the self-deception of those who have believed us less able to endure misfortune with fortitude than to encounter danger with courage. We have now entered upon a new phase of the struggle, the memory of which is to endure for all ages and to shed an increasing luster upon our country. Relieved from

the necessity of guarding cities and particular points, important but not vital to our defense; with an army free to move from point to point and strike in detail the garrisons and detachments of the enemy; operation in the interior of the country, where supplies are more accessible and where the foe will be far removed from his own base and cut off from all succor in case of reverse, nothing is needed to render our triumph certain, but the exhibition of our own unquenchable resolve. Let us but will it, and we are free, and who, in the light of the past dare doubt your purpose in the future. Antimated by that confidence in your spirit and fortitude which never yet has failed me, I announce to you, fellow countrymen, that it is my purpose to maintain your cause with my whole heart and soul; that I will never consent to abandon to the enemy one foot of the soil of any of the States of the Confederacy.... If by stress of numbers we should be compelled to a temporary withdrawal from [Virginia's] limits or those of any other border state, again and again we will return, until the baffled exhausted enemy shall abandon in despair his endless and impossible task of making slaves of people resolved to be free. Let us not then despond, my countrymen, but relying on the neverfailing mercies and protecting care of our God, let us meet the foe with fresh defiance, with unconquered and unconquerable hearts.[55]

It was an unbelieveable statement. The whole concept of the Confederacy was a fight for what it saw as decency, for home and family. Here was President Jefferson Davis calling on the troops to enter a new phase of war; to become roving bands attacking the enemy and then retreating to hide. Many fights for freedom began as guerrilla operations and turned into legitimate governments, but Davis proposed to turn a legitimate government into a guerrilla band. The people of the Confederacy would never accept this, but Davis did not seem to know, and he made a final flight from reality when he suggested that the Union troops would somehow become baffled and exhausted, this from the leader of the nation that was itself totally baffled and exhausted. Davis had still not heard from Lee and had no way of knowing that on that same day, Abraham Lincoln was sitting in the chair Davis had occupied for four years in the president's house in Richmond.

Just 100 miles away, an artillery staff officer talked with Lee and offered the same advice Davis had given in his proclamation. The officer told Lee that the men should take to the hills like "rabbits and partridges" in order to fight on against the Union. Lee listened quietly but quickly rejected the advice. "The men would not fight that way," he began, "their homes have been overrun, and many would go to look after their families. We must consider its effect on the country as a whole. Already it is demoralized by four years of war. If I took your advice, the men would be without rations and under no control of officers. They would be compelled to rob and steal in order to live. They would become mere bands of marauders and the enemy's cavalry would pursue them and overrun many sections they may never have occasion to visit."[56] Lee and Davis were out of touch and had no way of knowing that they were giving conflicting views on the future course of the war.

Tuesday afternoon, Davis met with Semmes to discuss the effort to gather supplies for Lee's army. Davis clung to the hope that Lee would be arriving soon and would need food and ammunition. But the need was more immediate than that. Lee had arrived at Amelia Court House where he expected to find rations for his men. He desperately needed 350,000 rations to keep his army going. Some 28,000 men had followed Lee from the trenches of Petersburg, but only half that number remained three days later. The men had not eaten for days but the breakdown of the Confederate government was nearly complete and there were no supplies for Lee's men. They were forced to scrounge for food. Lee would later say that the lack of supplies forced a delay that "was fatal and could not be retrieved."[57] But in Danville, Davis was sitting on nearly two million rations that would never be used.

On Wednesday, Davis wrote to his wife

> I have in vain sought to get into communication with General Lee, and have postponed writing in the hope that I would soon be able to speak to you with some confidence of the future.... I do not wish to leave Virginia, but cannot decide on my movements until those of the army are better developed.[58]

There was little for Davis or the Cabinet to do in Danville. In this vacuum some Confederate leaders began to dream; perhaps Lee had scored a military victory over Grant and the Union Army was on the defensive. Mallory later wrote, "To a few, very few, they were days of hope; to the many, they were days of despondency, if not despair; and to all, days of intense anxiety."[59] Haw, of the Ordnance Department, called the week "a season of suspense."[60]

Many of Semme's men were not needed on the fortifications and they gathered at the newly established Naval Store to write letters. Some fished in the Dan River and Benjamin spent long hours discussing his favorite poet Tennyson with his roommate Hoge.

Postmaster Reagan set up a post office in the Masonic Hall and began processing letters. The Confederate treasury had been divided, half being stored in the Bank of Danville, the rest remaining on the train under the guard of the midshipmen.

On Thursday, Lee's Army of Northern Virginia fought its last major battle. The Army was crossing the Appomattox River in its continuing retreat from Grant, when the troops became separated and before Lee realized what was happening, the Army was cut in half. The Union troops moved between the split columns and captured a third of the men Lee had left.

Also on Thursday, Danville began to get its first indication of how things were going in the field. Stragglers from Lee's army began drifting into town carrying the news that things were not going well. That night, Davis wrote his wife, "We are now fixing an executive office where the current business may be transacted here."[61]

On Friday, Grant sent a message to Lee saying, "The result of the last week must convince you of the hopelessness of further resistance on the part of the Army of Northern Virginia."[62] Lee received Grant's message but continued his drive toward Appomattox Court House. He crossed the Appomattox River, but his men were unable to burn the bridges and now he was trapped between two large Federal armies and decided to reply to Grant's message.

> I have received your note of this date. Though not entertaining the opinion you express of the hopelessness of further resistance on the part of the Army of Northern Virginia, I reciprocate your desire to avoid useless effusion of blood, and therefore, before considering your proposition, ask the terms you will offer on condition of its surrender.[63]

Grant received the reply on Saturday and immediately sent a response.

> Peace being my great desire there is but one condition I would insist upon, namely that the men and officers shall be disqualified from taking up arms again against the Government of the United States until properly exchanged."[64]

Grant offered to meet with Lee to receive the surrender. Late in the afternoon, Lee replied to Grant,

> I did not intend to propose the surrender of the
> Army of Northern Virginia, but to ask the terms of your
> proposition. To be frank, I do not think the emergency
> has arisen to call for the surrender of this army; but
> as the restoration of peace should be the sole object of
> all, I desired to know whether your proposals would
> lead to that end. I cannot, therefore, meet you with a
> view to surrender the Army of Northern Viriginia;
> but as far as your proposal may affect the C.S. forces
> under my command, & tend to the restoration of peace,
> I should be pleased to meet you at ten a.m. tomorrow,
> on the old stage road to Richmond, between the picket
> lines of the two armies.[65]

Saturday night, Lee called his final council of war asking his aides their opinions. Their only chance, they agreed, was to break through the Union troops, an impossible feat, but the only option remaining.

Lee also dispatched Lieutenant John S. Wise to ride to Danville to inform Davis of the situation. Lee gave Wise a piece of paper allowing him to make an oral report to Davis. "I fear to write, lest you be captured, for those people* are already several miles above Farmville. You must keep on the north side to a ford eight miles above here, and be careful about crossing even there."

Saturday evening, Davis and his Cabinet met in the dining room of the Sutherlin home. Wise arrived shortly after eight p.m. with the message from Lee. Wise stood at one end of the long table, looking directly at Davis seated at the other end. He began by saying that the Army had retreated too far west and could not turn south to Danville. "In my opinion,

*Lee did not refer to the Union troops as the enemy but as "those people."

Mr. President, it is only a question of a few days," Wise said. It was certainly not the news the Cabinet expected to hear. They began firing questions at Wise, who was tired and made his replies in a quiet, flat voice. Finally, Davis asked if Lee's army could reach a place of safety. Wise answered, "No, from what I saw and heard, I am satisfied that General Lee must surrender ... if I may be permitted to add a word, I think the sooner the better ... to spare the useless effusion of ... blood."

Davis was stunned and the other Cabinet members shuddered. Davis chose to ignore the Lieutenant's advice, and the Cabinet members — no matter what they may have thought privately — supported him. Davis said nothing of the message to his hosts in Danville.

Wise later wrote, "I remember the expression of face — almost a shutter — with which what I saw was received. I saw that, however convinced they might be of the truth of it, it was not a popular speech to make."[66]

Sunday morning, April 9, Danville leaders held a special church service at the Episcopal Church on Main Street to show support for the Confederate government. Throughout the city, church bells rang.

But near Appomattox Station, the end was coming for Lee's army. At dawn, the Confederates attacked in hopes of breaking through the Federal lines, using what remained of the cavalry. For a brief moment, it looked as if they might make their escape. But as the Confederates broke through the Union cavalry, they found what Lee feared most, Union infantry. Lee was trapped and escape was impossible. He heard the news and turned to an aide saying, "It would be useless and therefore cruel to provoke the further effusion of blood, and I have arranged to meet with General Grant with a view to surrender...." Grant replied that he could not discuss peace terms, only surrender. Lee replied, "I ask a suspension of hostilities pending the adjustment of the terms of the surrender of this army, in the interview requested in my former communication. today."[67]

Early Sunday afternoon, Grant and Lee met at Appomattox Court House in the home of Wilmer McLean, who had lived near the site of the battle of First Bull Run, then moved to Appomattox in hopes of getting away from the war. Lee surrendered his army of less than 10,000 men and told them, "I have done for you all that it was in my power to do. You have done your duty. Leave the results to God. Go to your homes and resume your occupations. Obey the laws and become as good citizens as you were soldiers."[68]

In Danville, Davis returned from church in good spirits. Four days earlier, Lee had sent a message to Davis saying, "I shall be tonight at Farmville, You can communicate by telegraph to Meherrin and by courier to Lynchburg."[69] But Davis did not receive the message until Sunday and replied immediately with a message of his own, hours after Lee had surrendered.

> I had hoped to have seen you at an earlier period, and trust soon to meet you.... We have here provisions and clothing for your Army, and they are held for its use.... I hope soon to hear from you at this point, where offices have been opened to keep up the current business, until more definite knowledge would enable us to form more permanent plans. May God preserve, sustain and guide you."[70]

Sunday night, Davis had dinner with Major and Mrs. Sutherlin, still unaware that Lee had surrendered. At one point, Mrs. Sutherlin asked Davis if the war would be over should Lee surrender. "By no means," the President replied, "We'll fight it out to the Mississippi River."[71]

Monday morning dawned with heavy grey clouds in the sky in Danville, and brought with it the first indications that the end was at hand. Admiral Semmes wrote in his memoirs, "The first news we received of his surrender, came to us from the stream of fugitives which now came pressing into our lines at Danville. It was heartrendering to look upon these men, some on foot, some on horseback, some nearly famished for want of food, and others barely able to totter along from disease. It was, indeed, a rabble rout."[72]

Early Monday afternoon, Davis took a carriage to the Benedict house to confer with his fellow government officials. He had planned to stay at the house a short time, but rain began falling and quickly turned into a violent storm. He decided to remain for dinner and relaxed as the meal was prepared in what had been the kitchen for a girl's school. At 3:30, Captain W.P. Graves, a messenger from Lee, arrived at the headquarters of General Harrison Walker, who commanded some 3,000 troops in and around Danville. Harrison sent Graves to the Benedict house, where Graves found Davis and handed him a brief note. Davis read the report and sat very still, then turned pale. Mallory wrote that the "news fell upon the ears of all like a fire bell in the night.... They [Cabinet members] carefully scanned the message as it passed from hand to hand, looked at each other gravely and mutely, and for some moments a silence more eloquent of great disaster than words could have been, prevailed. The importance of prompt action, however, was evident, and in a short time preparations for moving South before the enemy cavalry could intervene and prevent escape, was in rapid progress."[73]

IV. Flight to Greensboro

The people of Danville had clearly enjoyed the short-lived honor of being the capital of the Confederacy. But with Lee's army beaten, it became clear that the Union forces would now come after Davis. They knew what had happened to Richmond just one week before and now feared that their city would be next. It was time for the Confederate government to move on once again. The move from Richmond to Danville had some reasoning behind it, even if it was faulty: remain on Virginia soil, as a symbol, and wait for Lee's army. But now, the government had no place to go if it moved.

And yet Davis had a problem. He was a strict constitutionalist and the Confederate Constitution made no provision for dissolving the nation. Generals could surrender armies, but he could not simply shut down the Confederacy like an unsuccessful merchant closes down a store. Perhaps the states could take the action, maybe even the Confederate Congress, but he could not.

Davis quickly studied a map of what remained of the Confederacy and decided that Charlotte would be a safe, if temporary, haven. General William Sherman's troops were moving into North Carolina chasing General Joseph Johnston's army and he certainly would not turn south to seek out Davis. The easiest route would be through Greensboro.

On Sunday, Davis had sent a telegram to General P.G.T. Beauregard in Greensboro telling him to bring his men to Danville to help the city's defenses. Now, one day later, he sent Beauregard a second telegram telling him to stay in Greensboro.

Benjamin returned to his residence to pack and found the Rev. Hoge talking with two women. He talked briefly with the three, then pulled Hoge aside saying, "I did not have the heart to tell those good ladies what I have just learned. General Lee has surrendered and I fear the Confederate cause is lost."[74]

Davis returned to the Sutherlin house to prepare for the trip to Greensboro. Virginia Governor William "Extra Billy" Smith arrived at the house late Monday and learned of Lee's retreat for the first time from Davis who said, "Well sir, though unofficial. I have no doubt of the fact. You see my people packing up and I shall be off as soon as possible."

About 9:30 p.m., as Davis prepared to leave the Sutherlin house for the train station, Mrs. Sutherlin came to him and offered him a small bag of gold. With tears in his eyes, Davis said, "No, I cannot take your money. You and your husband are young and will need your money, while I am old and don't reckon I shall need anything very long." Instead, Davis gave her a small gold pencil he carried.[75]

At ten, Davis and his Cabinet gathered at the Danville station, where they found a mass of humanity frantically trying to board the Davis train. A few men were seeking to join Johnston's army to continue the fight, others were seeking to get out of Danville by any means. Davis and anyone who looked like a government official was surrounded by anxious citizens and soldiers seeking a seat. Colonel Burton Harrison, after accompanying Mrs. Davis to Charlotte, had rejoined Davis in Danville and was put in charge of the evacuation. But he was no match for the job, the rain poured down and loading supplies onto the train was difficult as the crowd rushed to grab anything of value.

Treasury Secretary Trenholm's condition had grown worse and he was carried to the train in an ambulance. Mallory would later write, "Nothing seemed to be ready or in order, and the train, with the President, did not leave until nearly eleven o'clock. Much rain had fallen and the depot could be reached only through mud knee deep. With utter darkness, the crowding of quartermaster's wagons, the yells of their contending drivers, the curses, loud and deep, of soldiers, organized and disorganized, determined to get upon in defiance of the guard, the mutual shouts of inquiry and response as to missing individuals or baggage, the want of baggage arrangements, the insufficient and dangerous provision made for getting horses into their cars, the crushing of the crowd, and the determination to get transportation at any hazzard, together with the absence of any recognized authority, all seasoned by sub rosa rumors that the enemy had already cut the Greensboro road, created a confusion such as it was never before the fortune of old Danville to witness."[76]

Spencer, the Negro servant who had somehow managed to board the Davis train from Richmond despite the objections of the President, showed up at the Danville depot but announced that he would not be going on the train. Apparently, during the ride to Danville, Spencer had encountered an old enemy on the train and had feared that the man might harm him if he saw him again. But Spencer later learned that his enemy would not be on the train and he asked

49

Harrison for a seat. Harrison told him to ride in the baggage car with the explosives, but Spencer declined, shaking his head and saying, "Marse Jeff will have to take care of himself."

Harrison was approached by a general from the torpedo department with his daughters in tow. The general sought seats for himself and his family and freight space for some of his explosives. Harrison said no, but the general, an old friend, obtained permission to board from President Davis.

Before Davis would leave, he insisted on writing letters of appreciation to the mayor and city council of Danville. He wrote Mayor J.M. Walker thanking him for "your generous reception of myself and the Executive officers who accompanied me. The shadows of misfortune which were on us when I came have become darker, and I trust you accord to me now, as then, your good wishes and confidence."

The delay to allow Davis to write the letters came as a distraction but no surprise to his aides. Earlier in the day he had taken time to interview Andrew Kercheval, a man seeking a job as a telegraph station supervisor.

Finally, the demand for seats on the train became so great that the ten original cars were overcrowded and two additional cars were added over the protests of the trainmen. The train lurched forward, then stopped. Again, it lurched forward and this time traveled nearly five miles before coming to a stop. The weight of the cars was too much for the engine and a cylinder had broken. Another engine was quickly brought up and the train moved on.

One of the daughters of the general from the torpedo bureau sat down next to Davis and began chatting. Davis sat motionless while she talked about the weather and her dresses and shot dozens of questions at Davis. Her voice could be heard throughout the car, since she was the only one talking. As she talked, Davis did not notice that the train moved out of Virginia, the state Davis had promised never to leave.

50

In the midst of her chattering, there was a sharp explosion near Davis, and everyone in the car quickly jumped fearing the worst. A young man, assigned to the general from the torpedo bureau grabbed the seat of his pants with both hands and it turned out that he had an explosive device in his pocket that went off when he sat on a stove in the car.[77]

Back in Danville, two companies of soldiers had been left behind to protect the food and ammunition left by the government. No sooner had the Davis train departed than a crowd began to gather at the storehouse. Finally, a woman yelled, "Our children and we'uns are starving; the Confederacy is gone up; let us help ourselves." The guards were pushed away and the storehouses looted. In the midst of the looting, the nearby ammunition train exploded, killing 50 civilians and soldiers.

Elsewhere in Danville other sorry dramas were being played out. Joseph Haw, the Ordnance Department clerk, recalled seeing, "an elderly man, too old for military service, [who] evidently had come from his home in North Carolina with boxes for men of a North Carolina regiment. Finding he could not reach them, he was selling the contents of the boxes at auction. It was a pitiful and pathetic scene. He would hold up a string of dried pumpkins and cry, 'How much for this?' or a poke of beans or peas, a large cake of gingerbread, a few apples or black walnuts, a piece of bacon or a pair of homemade knit socks, until the box was sold out, then go through another."[78]

Davis, who had promised to continue the fight with "fresh defiance," now clung to the hope that Johnston would be able to defeat Sherman, then turn and defeat Grant. This was the same Joe Johnston whose army had been running from Sherman across four states. Davis hinted that the new capital of the Confederacy would be set up in Texas.

At Appomattox, Lee issued his last general order:

After four years of arduous service, marked by unsurpassed courage and fortitude, the Army of Northern Virginia has been compelled to yield to overwhelming numbers and resources. I need not tell the brave survivors of so many hard fought battles, who had remained steadfast to the last, that I have consented to the result from no distrust of them. But feeling that valor and devotion could accomplish nothing that would compensate for the loss that must have attended the continuance of the contest, I have determined to avoid the useless sacrifice of those whose past services have endeared them to their countrymen. By the terms of the agreement officers and men can return to their homes and remain until exchanged. You will take with you the satisfaction that proceeds from the consciousness of duty faithfully performed, and I earnestly pray that a Merciful God will extend to you His blessings and protection. With an increasing admiration of your constancy and devotion to your country, and a grateful remembrance of your kind and generous considerations for myself, I bid you all an affectionate farewell.[79]

Lee and Grant held another meeting and Grant urged Lee to call on the remaining Confederate armies to surrender, but Lee said that decision was up to Davis.

While Davis fled South, there were two other escape adventures being played out. The Confederate gold, under the command of Captain Parker and his sixty midshipmen, had left Danville on April 6, a Thursday. Parker stayed in Greensboro for one day, then decided to head South again. He left behind $35,000 for Davis, $39,000 for Johnston's army and took the rest on to Charlotte, where he deposited it in the Confederate mint. But Parker had strong fears about the safety of the gold. Rumors had circulated about the treasure and with each retelling the size grew. Parker feared that Confederate soldiers, convinced they were entitled to the money, or Union troops, would seize it. He removed the treasure from the mint and had it placed aboard a train, hidden beneath a supply of sugar, coffee, bacon and flour he obtained from the naval storehouse in Charlotte.[80]

Parker was also worried about the safety of Mrs. Davis, who was still in Charlotte. He convinced her to join his treasure train and move South. Just as Davis entered Greensboro, Parker, Mrs. Davis and the treasure left Charlotte by train. The guard had been enlarged by the addition of men from the Portsmouth Navy Yard, and there were now nearly 150 men to guard the gold.

V. The Military Realities Close In

Aboard the train to Greensboro, Davis and his Cabinet sat quietly, knowing that Union raiders were in the area. The train arrived in Greensboro in the early morning hours and they were met with the news that General George Stoneman's cavalry had burned a railroad bridge shortly after their train had passed. For the first time in weeks Davis smiled, and said, "A miss is as good as a mile."[81]

In Richmond, Davis had been treated with the utmost respect; even with the war going badly, the citizens knew that Davis had given his all. They had seen him put his own possessions up for public auction and knew that the war had cost him his health and wealth. In Danville, every courtesy had been extended; Davis was, after all, still the President. But in Greensboro, the mood was different. The Confederacy had all but ceased to exist and Davis had crossed the line from leader of a nation to hunted criminal. Greensboro residents knew that Sherman's troops had leveled Atlanta and

Columbia and with Davis in their city, the force of the Union army might be brought to bear on them. Fearing reprisals for any consideration given to Davis, the city gave none.

Greensboro had been a center of anti-Confederate sentiment during the war and leading citizens had turned out for pro-Union meetings, even petitioning their state government to make peace with the North. Now, the residents were beginning the long task of putting the war behind them as they turned to the more pressing needs of finding food or anxiously awaiting the return of relatives from the army. Mallory called the treatment given Davis a "pitiable phase of human nature."[82]

Davis and his Cabinet, with the exception of the seriously ill Trenholm, had no place to stay. John Motley Morehead, one of the city's richest and most important men, met the train and offered to let Trenholm stay in his home, but his motives were entirely selfish. Colonel Harrison said, "This hospitality was explained by the information that the host was the alarmed owner of many of the bonds, and of much of the currency, of the Confederate States, and that he hoped to cajole the Secretary into exchanging a part of the 'treasured gold' for some of those securities. It appeared that we were reported to have many millions of gold with us."[83]

One of the President's aides, Colonel John Taylor Wood, a nephew of Davis' first wife, had moved his family to Greensboro several weeks earlier and found them a place to stay in a boarding house. Wood offered Davis a room in the house over the objections of the owner, who feared revenge from Stoneman's cavalry. The other residents were also unhappy about the arrangement and were even more upset when government officials began dropping by for conferences, calling attention to the situation. Davis' quarters consisted of a bed, a single chair and a small table in a room measuring twelve by sixteen feet.[84]

The other Cabinet members set up housekeeping in the train, converting the dilapidated coaches into sleeping quarters. Most of their time was spent in a leaky boxcar they nicknamed the "Cabinet Car." From the Navy Store they drew rations of bread and bacon, but were forced to forage for eggs, coffee and flour. They ate from tin plates and used tin cups for spoons. The collapse of the Confederacy had left them with little to do and they spent most of their time exchanging stories and jokes. Mallory described the Cabinet members sitting around a small table: "Here was the astute Minister of Justice, a grave and most exemplary gentleman, with a piece of half-boiled 'middling' in one hand and a hoecake in the other, his face beaming unmistakeable evidence of the condition of the bacon. There was the clever Secretary of State busily dividing his attention between a bucket of dried apples and a haversack of hard-boiled eggs. Here was a postmaster-general sternly and energetically running his bowie knife through a ham as if it were the chief business of life; and there was the Secretary of the Navy courteously swallowing his coffee scalding hot that he might not keep the venerable Adjutant-General waiting too long for the coveted tin cup! All personal discomforts were not only borne with cheerful philosophy, but were made the constant texts for merry comment, quaint anecdotes, or curious story. State sovereignty, secession, ... and other ... recurring and fruitful themes of discussion, gave place to the more pressing and practical questions of dinner or no dinner, and how, when and where it was to be had, and to schemes and devices for enabling a man of six feet to sleep upon a car four feet long."[85]

On Wednesday, Mobile, the largest city still in Confederate hands, fell to the Union. Sherman was approaching Raleigh and encountering little resistance from Johnston.

General Beauregard and his staff had arrived Tuesday evening and found lodging in three boxcars near the

Cabinet cars. As soon as Beauregard arrived, Davis called him to the presidential train for news of Johnston's troops. Beauregard told of Johnston's hurried evacuation of Smithfield and said Johnston did not plan to defend Raleigh. In short, Beauregard said the situation was hopeless, but Davis would not accept that. He clung to the hope that part of Lee's army had survived Appomattox and was even now pushing toward North Carolina to join Johnston in the final battle against Sherman. Beauregard was shocked, but could not change Davis' opinion. Davis thought for a moment, then decided to call Johnston to Greensboro for a strategy conference. The military was obviously ready to give up, but if he could only talk directly to the generals, he could convince them that there was hope. "The important question first to be solved is what point of concentration should be made," Davis told Beauregard. Almost as an afterthought, Davis turned to Beauregard and admitted, "your intimate knowledge of the date for the solution of the problem deters me from making specific suggestions on the point."[86]

Johnston arrived the next morning, Wednesday, April 5, and took up residence in one of Beauregard's boxcars. Beauregard would later write, "We supposed that we were to be questioned concerning the military resources of our department in connection with the question of continuing or terminating the war." Instead, "The President's object seemed to be to give, not obtain information."[87]

Davis was full of ideas for winning the war. He suggested raising a new army comprised of deserters and drafting men who had successfully avoided the draft for four years. Both Beauregard and Johnston quickly protested that men who had refused to serve when things were going well for the South would hardly rush to serve the falling flag. Finally, Johnston came to his most pressing concern; he wanted permission to open negotiations with Sherman. Davis said no, if the talks failed—as he was sure they would—"its failure would have a demoralizing effect on both the troops and the people. Neither of them had shown any disposition to surrender, or had any reason to suppose that their government contemplated abandoning its trust."[88]

Davis said he was aware of "our present condition and the gravity of our position." But he later wrote, "I did not think we should despair. We still had effective armies in the field, and a vast extent of rich and productive territory both east and west of the Mississippi, whose citizens had evinced no disposition to surrender. Ample supplies had been collected in the railroad depots, and much still remained to be placed at our disposal when needed by the army in North Carolina."[89]

The table fell silent. An impasse had been reached and as the three men had nothing more to talk about, they all sat stonefaced. At last, Davis broke the silence and said that Breckinridge was expected to arrive at any moment with information about the condition of Lee's army and he suggested a recess until Breckinridge arrived. Beauregard and Johnston quickly accepted the reprieve.

Lee had remained near Appomattox Court House and on Wednesday sent a long letter to Davis, explaining the events of the past week.

> It is with pain that I announce to Your Excellency the surrender of the Army of Northern Virginia. The operations which preceded this result will be reported in full. I will therefore only now state that upon arriving at Amelia Court House on the morning of the 4th with the advance of the army, on its retreat from the lines in front of Richmond and Petersburg, and not finding the supplies ordered to be placed there, nearly twenty-four hours were lost in endeavoring to collect in the country subsistence for men and horses. This delay was fatal, and could not be retrieved. The

troops, wearied by continued fighting and marching for
several days and nights, obtained neither rest nor re-
freshment; and on moving on the 5th on the Richmond
and Danville Railroad, I found at Jetersville the
enemy's cavalry, and learned the approach of his
infantry and the general advance of his army towards
Burkeville. This deprived us of the use of the railroad,
and rendered it impracticable to procure from Danville
the supplies ordered to meet us at points of our march.
Nothing could be obtained from the adjacent country.
Our route on the Roanoke was therefore changed, and
the march directed upon Farmville, where supplies
were ordered from Lynchburg. The change of route
threw the troops on the roads pursued by the artillery
and wagon trains west of the railroad, which impeded
our advance and embarrassed our movements. On the
morning of the 6th Genl [James] Longstreet's corps
reached Rice's Station on the Lynchburg Railroad. It
was followed by the commands of Genls R.H. Anderson, Ewell, and [John] Gordon, with orders to close
upon it as fast as the progress of the trains would permit
or as they could be directed (diverted) on roads farther
west. Genl Anderson, commanding Pickett's and B.R.
Johnson's divisions, became disconnected with [Gen.
William] Mahone's division, forming the rear of Longstreet. The enemy's cavalry penetrated the line of march
through the interval thus left and attacked the wagon
moving towards Farmville. This caused serious delay in
the march of the center and rear of the column, and enabled the enemy to mass upon their flank. After successive
attacks Anderson's and [Gen. Richard] Ewell's corps were
captured or driven from their position. The latter general,
with both of his division commanders, [Gen. Joseph] Kershaw and Custis Lee, and his brigardiers, were taken
prisoners. Gordon, who all the morning, aided by Genl
W.H.F. Lee's cavalry, had checked the advance of the
enemy on the road from Amelia Springs and protected the
trains, became exposed to his combined assaults, which he
bravely resisted and twice repulsed; but the cavalry having been withdrawn to another part of the line of march,

and the enemy massing heavily on his front and both flanks, renewed the attack about six p.m., and drove him from the field in much confusion. The army continued its march during the night, and every effort was made to reorganize the divisions which had been shattered by the day's operations. But the men depressed by fatigue and hunger, many threw away their arms, while others followed the wagon trains and embarrassed their progress. On the morning of the 7th rations were issued to the troops as they passed Farmville, but the safety of the trains requiring their removal upon the approach of the enemy, all could not be supplied. The army reduced to two corps under Longstreet and Gordon, moved steadily on the road to Appomattox Court House. Thence its march was ordered by Campbell Court House through Pittsylvania towards Danville. The roads were wretched and the progress of the trains slow. By great efforts the head of the column reached Appomattox Court House on the evening of the 8th, and the troops were halted for rest. The march was ordered to be resumed by one a.m. on the 9th. Fitz Lee with the cavalry, supported by Gordon, was ordered to drive the enemy from his front, wheel to the left, and cover the passage of the trains, while Longstreet, who from Rice's station had formed the rear guard, should close up and hold the position. Two battalions of artillery and the ammunition wagons were directed to accompany the army. The rest of the artillery and wagons to move towards Lynchburg. In the early part of the night the enemy attacked [Gen. R.L.] Walker's artillery train near Appomattox Station on the Lynchburg Railroad, and were repelled. Shortly afterwards their cavalry dashed towards the Court House till halted by our line. During the night there were indications of a large force massing on our left and front. Fitz Lee was directed to ascertain its strength, and to suspend his advance till daylight if necessary. About five a.m. on the 9th, with Gordon on his left, he moved forward and opened the war. A heavy force of the enemy was discovered opposite Gordon's right, which,

61

moving in the direction of Appomattox Court House, drove back the left of the cavalry and threatened to cut off Gordon from Longstreet. His cavalry at the same time threatening to envelop his left flank, Gordon withdrew across the Appomattox River, and the cavalry advanced on the Lynchburg road and became separated from the army. Learning the condition of affairs on the lines, where I had gone under the expectation of meeting Genl Grant to learn definitely the terms he proposed in a communication received from him on the 8th, in the event of the surrender of the army. I requested a suspension of hostilities until these terms could be arranged. In the interview which occurred with Genl Grant in compliance with my request, terms having been agreed on, I surrendered that portion of the Army of Northern Virginia which was on the field, with its arms, artillery, and wagon trains; the officers and men to be paroled, retaining their side arms and private effects. I deemed this course the best under all the circumstances by which we were surrounded. On the morning of the 9th, according to the reports of the ordnance officers, there were seven thousand eight hundred and ninety two organized infantry with arms, with an average of seventy-five round of ammunition per man. The artillery, though reduced to sixty-three pieces, with ninety-three rounds of ammunition, was sufficient. These comprised all the supplies of ordnance that could be relied on in the State of Virginia. I have no accurate report of the cavalry, but believe it did not exceed two thousand and one hundred effective men. The enemy was more than five times our numbers. If we could have forced our way one day longer it would have been at a great sacrifice of life; at its end, I did not see how a surrender could have been avoided. We had no subsistence for man or horse, and it could not be gathered in the country. The supplies ordered to Pamlin's Station from Lynchburg could not reach us, and the men deprived of food and sleep for many days, were worn out and exhausted.[90]

The Military Realities Close In

Breckinridge arrived Wednesday evening and went directly to a private meeting with Beauregard and Johnston. He had ridden on horseback from Richmond and was exhausted. He brought only one piece of information, but it was significant: Lee's entire army down to the last man had surrendered. There would be no help coming for Johnston's embattled army. Breckinridge told Beauregard and Johnston that any attempt to continue the war would "be the greatest of human crimes."[91] Johnston said he agreed, but the question was, could they get Davis to listen?

On Thursday morning at ten, Davis convened a meeting of his Cabinet and military leaders in the grim little room Davis was calling home. Reagan would later call the atmosphere "most solemnly funeral."[92] Trenholm was too ill to attend and the room was divided into three groups. Jefferson Davis and Benjamin still seeing hope for victory, the other Cabinet members except for Breckinridge remaining neutral and the military leaders advocating an end to the war as quickly as possible. Before leaving Richmond, Davis had hoped that Lee and Johnston would be able to join forces and defeat the enemy, even after Lee surrendered, Davis clung to the idea that some of his men had escaped to fight again. Now, with the news that Lee's entire army had laid down its guns, Davis decided that it really didn't matter. "Our late disasters are terrible, but I do not think we should regard them as fatal. I think we can whip the enemy yet, if our people will turn out." He paused briefly, waiting for some indication of support, but none came and he looked down quietly and said, "We should like to hear your views, General Johnston."

Here was the chance Johnston had been waiting for. Davis and Johnston had become increasingly bitter enemies after Davis removed him from command in Atlanta in 1864. It was a feud that would continue for the rest of their lives.

63

Now, Johnston had his chance to speak his mind and his voice was bitter. Mallory would describe it as spiteful.

"My views are, sir, that our people are tired of war, feel themselves whipped, and will not fight." He could have stopped there, but the hate was too great and the words tumbled out. He said the Confederacy was "without money, or credit, or army, or ammunition, or means of procuring them. My men are daily deserting in large numbers. Since Lee's defeat they regard the war as at an end." He said there was no choice but surrender. "We may perhaps obtain terms which we ought to accept." He said continuing the war would not harm the enemy but would "complete the devastation of our country and ruin of its people."

Davis listened without expression. His eyes were fixed downward on a small piece of paper he repeatedly folded and unfolded. There was a brief silence when Johnston finished and then Davis said, "What do you say, General Beauregard?" Beauregard, another enemy of Davis, said only, "I concur in all General Johnston has said." There was another silence as Davis continued to toy with his small piece of paper. Without looking up, Davis said, "You speak of obtaining terms." The words hung in the air for a moment before Johnston said he would like to contact Sherman to arrange a truce to begin working out the details for surrender. With the exception of Benjamin, those in the room now backed the generals. Davis said, "Well, sir, you can adopt this course, though I am not sanguine as to the ultimate results." But he had agreed that the talks could begin. Sherman was now only fifty miles from Greensboro.[93]

In Washington, Lincoln met with his Cabinet and told them of his plans for the reconstruction of the South. He urged a policy of forgiveness toward the South. Lincoln had some confidence that he would not have to decide what to do with the leaders of the Confederacy, saying he hoped they "would flee" to foreign countries. In fact, Lincoln made it clear that he would have no objections if the Confederate leaders received some unofficial Union aid in their flight.

In Greensboro, Davis was thinking of flight, but not to a foreign nation. He was confident that Johnston's negotiations with Sherman would fail and the government in exile would once again have to continue its flight. Others might talk of surrender, but not Davis. Again and again, he said he had "no idea whatsoever of leaving Confederate soil as long as there are men in uniform to fight for the cause."[94]

On Friday, he wrote to his wife,

> Dear Winnie,
> I will come to you if I can. Everything is dark. You should prepare for the worst by dividing your baggage as to move in wagons.... I have lingered on the road to little purpose. My love to the children and Maggie. God bless, guide and preserve you, Your most affectionate, Banny."[95]

After leaving Charlotte, Mrs. Davis and the Confederate treasure had traveled to Chester, South Carolina, on April 13. Chester was the end of the railroad line and the baggage and treasure had to be transferred to wagons. While the moving took place, Mrs. Davis waited in the home of Brigadier General and Mrs. James Chestnut. Mrs. Chestnut wrote in her diary that, "Some people sent me things for Mrs. Davis, but there were people here so base as to be afraid to befriend Mrs. Davis, thinking that when the Yankees came, they would take vengeance on them for it. She left here at five o'clock. She was as calm and smiling as ever."[96]

Her party set off from Chester with Mrs. Davis and her children riding in an ambulance while most of the men walked. They had traveled a short distance when they came to a stretch of muddy road, bogging down the ambulance and forcing Mrs. Davis to walk. "The ambulance was too heavily laden in the deep mud and as my maid was too weak to walk and my nurse was unwilling, I walked five miles in the darkness in mud over my shoe tops, with my cheerful little baby in my arms." About one a.m., they arrived at the Woodward Baptist church, a small red brick building that used benches as pews. The exhausted group quickly placed their blankets on the benches and floor. Mrs. Davis was about to go to sleep on a bench, when the new bride of one of the bank officials guarding his bank's money came up to her. "We are lying on the floor, but have left the communion table for you out of respect."[97] Mrs. Davis said it would be in poor taste to sleep on the communion table and returned to her bench. Captain Parker slept in the pulpit.

The next morning, she had breakfast at the home of Mrs. Isaiah Mobley on the Ashford Ferry Road. They spent the night of April 14 at the plantation of Lieutenant Edward C. Means and the next day crossed the Broad River on a pontoon bridge. Parker was becoming more concerned about the safety of the treasure and began posting rear guards along the road.

Mrs. Davis arrived in Newberry, South Carolina, on Sunday, April 16, where the party transferred to a train for the journey to Abbeville. The Newberry newspaper carried reports of the surrender of General Lee, but quickly dismissed them as "an unmitigated falsehood of the enemy."[98]

66

VI. To Charlotte, Cut Off

Escape for Jefferson Davis and his Cabinet was becoming more difficult. Roving bands had begun raiding Confederate storehouses and the officials had difficulty obtaining food for the journey. The train line south had been destroyed by Union troops and the Davis party would have to use horses to continue their journey.

The departure from Greensboro was even more difficult than the departure from Danville. Thieves had begun stealing horses and raiding quartermaster stores. Chief Clerk Clark was finally able to put together enough horses and supplies for the journey south after several hours.

The size of the guard around Davis increased in Greensboro. An escort of Tennessee cavalry under the command of Brigadier General George G. Dribell and a company of Kentucky cavalry under Captain Given Campbell joined to act as guards and scouts.

Benjamin was becoming difficult to deal with, telling

Harrison that he would not mount a horse until he was forced to do so. Harrison, short and stout did not sit a horse well, and demanded an ambulance to ride in. With some difficulty, Harrison obtained ambulances, wagons and carriages for Benjamin, George Davis, Trenholm and Jefferson Davis, while Breckinridge, Mallory and Reagan rode horses.

"Heavy rains had recently fallen, the earth was saturated with water, the soil was sticky red clay, the mud was awful," Harrison wrote.[99] The refugees traveled at a slow pace as the vehicles became stuck in the mud. Harrison rode forward a few miles and found some artillery men camped and convinced them to ride back with him to rescue the stranded wagon. The wheels had to be levered out with fence rails.

The night was dark and the only light was the bright orange glow from the tip of Benjamin's cigar. At one point, the traveling party became grimly quiet, and Benjamin loudly launched into a recitation of Tennyson's ode on the death of the Duke of Wellington.

They had traveled just ten miles when they became so tired that they stopped to spend the night in the village of Jamestown. They found a nearby house and received their best treatment since leaving Virginia, eating a hearty meal and then being taken to the sleeping quarters. There was only one spare bedroom and everyone assumed that it would be given to Davis. As the men waited in the dark hallway, a Negro servant approached holding a candle. In the near darkness, he looked at the leaders of the Confederacy and then motioned for General [Samuel] Cooper to follow him. Cooper was escorted into the bedroom. The servant closed the door and one of the aides said to him, "Aren't you going to give the President a room?" The servant stared at the man in surprise and said, "Yes sir, I done put him in there.[100] The servant had decided that General Cooper looked more like a president than Davis. Another bed was found for Davis. As they slept, the night of the 14th, Lincoln was assassinated in Washington.

Saturday morning, the Davis party, cut off from all communication, arrived in High Point and then pushed on to Lexington, where they spent the night, sleeping in a pine grove outside the city. That evening, a messenger arrived from Johnston to brief Davis on the negotiations with Sherman. Davis dispatched Breckinridge and Reagan to go to Johnston's headquarters to take part in the talks. Later, North Carolina Governor Zebulon B. Vance arrived to talk with Davis. Vance was a Unionist before the war and refused to become a member of the Confederate Congress, instead joining the army. In 1862, at the age of thirty-two, he was elected governor.

The President invited Vance to attend a Cabinet meeting to discuss the future of the Confederacy and Vance later wrote that Davis expressed a "desire that I should accompany him, with such of the North Carolina troops as I might be able to influence to that end. He was very earnest and displayed a remarkable knowledge of the opinions and resources of the people of the Confederacy, as well as a most dauntless spirit." Vance said Davis spoke of "the possibility of retreating beyond the Mississippi with large sections of the soldiers still faithful to the Confederate cause, and resuming operations with General Kirby Smith's forces as a nucleus in those distant regions."

Vance said that after Davis spoke there was a silence. After several moments, several Cabinet members spoke in favor of the Davis plan and urged Vance to support the President. The last member to speak was Breckinridge who bluntly said that Davis was not being honest with Vance. Breckinridge said the Davis plan had so little chance of success as to be impractical and he advised Vance to remain in North Carolina. There was another silence around the table, then Davis looked at Breckinridge and said quietly, "Well, perhaps, General, you are right."

Vance rose and prepared to leave and Davis said, "God bless you, sir, and the noble old state of North Carolina."[101] Vance left and soon after Breckinridge and Reagan departed to join Johnston. Harrison would write that throughout the flight, Davis was "singularly equable and cheerful; he seemed to have a great load taken from his mind, to feel relieved of responsibilities, and his conversation was bright and agreeable. He talked of men and of books, particularly of Walter Scott and Byron; of horses, and dogs and sports, of the woods and the fields; of trees and plants, and of a variety of other topics."[102]

Leaving Lexington, Breckinridge, Mallory and Reagan rode horses. Jefferson Davis, not feeling well, rode in one ambulance and Trenholm in another. A third ambulance contained Benjamin and George Davis. The ambulances were pulled by old horses bleeding from mosquito bites, and they heaved and staggered and became bogged down in the mud. George Davis and an aide shoved fence rails beneath the wheels and the driver laid his whip on the horses, but to no avail. Harrison went looking for help and finally found a bivouacked artillery unit and persuaded them to come and help pull the ambulance from the mud.

The next day Davis and his party moved to Salisbury, North Carolina. As they crossed the Yadkin River over the railroad bridge, they kept a careful look out for Union cavalry that had raided Salisbury earlier. Davis and some of his aides stayed at the rectory of historic St. Luke's Episcopal Church as the guests of the Rev. Thomas G. Haughton. Harrison slept on the front porch of the rectory to guard Davis.

A Salisbury resident later wrote,

> It was at Salisbury where I first encountered Mr. Davis during that sad time at the home of the Episcopal

clergyman. About sunset, Mr. Davis, General Cooper, Colonel William Preston Johnston and one or two others of the President's staff came to the same house. At tea and after tea, Mr. Davis was cheerful, pleasant and inclined to talk. I remember we sat upon the porch until about ten o'clock, the President with an unlighted cigar in his mouth, talking of the misfortune of General Lee's surrender. On the following morning at breakfast, Mr. Davis sat at the left hand of the host. In the middle of the meal, the clergyman's little girl, a child of only seven or eight years, came in crying and greatly disturbed. She approached the table just between the President and her father and said: "Oh, Papa, old Lincoln's coming and going to kill us all." Mr. Davis at once laid down his knife and fork, and placing his right hand upon the child's head turned her tearful face toward his own and said with animation 'Oh, no, my little lady, you need not fear that. Mr. Lincoln is not such a bad man, he does not want to kill anybody, and certainly not a little girl like you.' The child was soon pacified and I shall never forget the kindly expression on the President's face.[103]

On Monday, Sherman met with Johnston at Durham Station, North Carolina. The fate of Johnston's army was clear; surrender was the only option. Johnston was also anxious to negotiate the surrender of Davis and the Cabinet, but Sherman wanted no part of that issue. The meeting ended with both sides agreeing to meet the following day.

Before daybreak on Tuesday, Breckinridge and Reagan met with Johnston. Reagan wrote down the terms discussed the previous day and Breckinridge went to meet with Sherman, who read the Confederate proposal, then drew up his own list of terms, which was not significantly different from the Confederate's.

The documents were signed and copies were sent to Jefferson Davis and the new United States president, Andrew

Johnson. General Johnston had agreed to surrender all of his remaining troops, but there was no mention of the Confederate leaders.

Johnston and Lee had now surrendered, Mobile was in Union hands and only General Kirby Smith had an army still intact, but he was in Texas, nearly a thousand miles from Davis, who continued to wind his way toward Charlotte. Davis had only covered thirty-six miles in two days since leaving Greensboro, a leisurely pace that surprised some of his aides.

Tuesday night, they slept in Concord at the home provided by Judge Victor C. Barringer.

Davis and his party were cut off from communication with fellow Southerners, who knew nothing of his movements. The Edgefield, South Carolina, *Advertiser* said, "We would like to inform our readers where these gentlemen (Davis and the Cabinet) are and what they are doing but we cannot.... We honor and trust him still, and hold the opinion that he will yet prove himself to be what we thought him when we placed him in the presidential chair." The Augusta, Georgia, *Constitutionalist* informed its readers that it had learned "on creditable authority" that the President had returned to Richmond to open negotiations with the North. And the *Richmond Evening Whig* said, "Great curiosity is naturally felt North and South to learn what has become of Jefferson Davis, the head of the greatest rebellion the world has yet seen...."[104]

On Wednesday, April 19, Davis and the Cabinet arrived in Charlotte, a city that had been a center for refugees throughout the war. Now, the city was overrun by paroled soldiers, deserters and stragglers. Coming into the city, Davis was met by Major General John Echols, who had arranged accommodations for some members of the Cabinet. Trenholm would stay with William F. Phifer, George Davis would stay with William Myers and Benjamin and Harrison would be housed by Mr. Weil, who had hosted Mrs. Davis earlier in the month.

But it was difficult to find a room for Davis. Finally, an L.F. Bates, agent for the Southern Express Company, offered Davis a room. Bates had a questionable reputation and Davis' aides were opposed to the President's staying there, but his option was to sleep in the streets.

As Davis entered the house, he received a message that Lincoln had been assassinated five days earlier.[105] Davis was stunned by the news, realizing that Lincoln would certainly be the best friend the South could have after the war.

There was little time to talk about the assassination because a column of Confederate cavalry arrived under the command of General Basil Duke. As they rode past the house where Davis was staying, they waved their battle flags and cheered the President. They stopped at the front door and began calling for Davis to speak. Davis thanked them for their cheers and expressed his own determination to fight on.

Davis had hoped that Charlotte would be willing to become the new capital of the Confederacy, but the city would have none of it.

Davis and his party remained in Charlotte for eight days, receiving conflicting advice on what to do next. He received a letter from Wade Hampton, who said the war could be won. "The military situation is very gloomy, I admit, but it is by no means desperate & endurance & determination will produce a change."[106] Hampton pledged that if he had just 20,000 men, he could defeat Sherman and Grant within twenty days. Hampton was dreaming, but it was the same dream Davis wanted desperately to believe.

On April 23, Davis wrote a long emotional letter to his wife, who was now in Abbeville, S.C.

> The dispersion of Lee's army and the surrender
> of the remnant which remained with him, destroyed

73

the hopes I had entertained when we parted. Had that
army held together, I am now confident we could have
successfully executed the plan which I sketched to you
and would have been today on the high road to independence. Even after that disaster, if the men who
"straggled," say thirty or forty thousand in number,
had come back with their arms and with a disposition
to fight we might have repaired the damage; but all
was sadly the reverse of that, they threw away theirs
and were uncontrollably resolved to go home. The
small guards along the road have sometimes been unable to prevent the pillage of trains and depots. Panic
has seized the country. J.E. Johnston and Beauregard
were hopeless as to recruiting their forces from the
dispersed men of Lee's army, and equally so as to their
ability to check Sherman with the forces they had.
Their only idea was to retreat. Of the power to do so
they were doubtful, and subsequent desertions from
their troops have materially diminished their strength,
and I learn still more weakened their confidence. The
loss of arms has been so great, that, should the spirit
of the people rise to the occasion, it would not be at
this time possible adequately to supply them with the
weapons of war.

     ...The issue is one which is very painful for me
to meet. On one hand is the long night of oppression
which will follow the return of our people to the
"Union"; on the other, the suffering of the women and
children, and carnage among the few brave patriots
who would still oppose the invader, and who, unless
the people would rise en-masse to sustain them, would
struggle but to die in vain. I think my judgment is undisturbed by any pride of opinion, I have prayed to
our Heavenly Father to give me wisdom and fortitude
equal to the demands of the position in which Provi-
dence has placed me. I have sacrificed so much for the
cause of the Confederacy that I can measure my ability
to make any further sacrifice required, and am assured
there is but one to which I am not equal — My wife and

my Children — How are they to be saved from degradation or want is now my care.

During the suspension of hostilities you may have the best opportunity to go to Mississippi, and there either to sail from Mobile for a foreign port or to cross the river and proceed to Texas, as the one or the other may be more practicable. The little sterling you have will be a very scanty store and under other circumstances would not be coveted, but if our land can be sold, that will secure you from absolute want. For myself, it may be that, a devoted band of Cavalry will cling to me, and that I can force my way across the Mississippi, and if nothing can be done there which it will be proper to do, then I can go to Mexico, and have the world from which to choose a location.

...Dear Wife, this is not the fate to which I invited [you] when the future was rose colored to us both; but I know you will bear it even better than myself, and that, of us two, I alone, will ever look back reproachfully on my past career.... Farewell, my dear, there may be better things in store for us than are now in view, but my love is all I have to offer, and that has the value of a thing long possessed and sure not to be lost...."[107]

But the most significant letter came from Lee:

The apprehensions I expressed during the winter of the moral condition of the Army of Northern Virginia, have been realized. The operations which occurred while the troops were in the entrenchments in front of Richmond and Petersburg were not marked by the boldness and decision which formerly characterized them. Except in particular instances, they were feeble; and a want of confidence seemed to possess officers and men. This condition, I think, was produced by the state of feeling in the country, and the communications received by the men from their homes, urging their return and the abandonment of the field. The movement

of the enemy on the 30th of March to Dinwiddie Court
House was consequently not as strongly met as similar
ones had been. Advantages were gained by him which
discouraged the troops, so that on the morning of the
2nd April, when our lines between the Appomattox
and Hatcher's Run were assaulted, the resistance was
not effectual: several points were penetrated and large
captures made. At the commencement of the withdrawal of the army from the lines on the night of the
2nd, it began to disintegrate, and straggling from the
ranks increased up to the surrender on the 9th. On that
day, as previously reported, there were only seven
thousand eight hundred and ninety-two effective infantry. During the night, when the surrender became
known more than ten thousand men came in, as
reported to me by the Chief Commissary of the Army.
During the succeeding days stragglers continued to give
themselves up, so that on the 12th April, according to
the rolls of those paroled, twenty-six thousand and
eighteen officers and men had surrendered. Men who
had left the ranks on the march, and crossed James
River, returned and gave themselves up, and many
have since come to Richmond and surrendered. I have
given these details that Your Excellency might know the
state of feelings which existed in the army, and judge of
that in the country. From what I have seen and learned,
I believe an army cannot be organized or supported in
Virginia, and as far as I know the condition of affairs,
the country east of the Mississippi is morally and
physically unable to maintain the contest unaided with
any hope of ultimate success. A partisan war may be
continued, and hostilities protracted, causing indi-
vidual suffering and the devastation of the country,
but I see no prospect by that means of achieving a separate independence. It is for Your Excellency to decide,
should you agree with me in opinion, what is proper to
be done. To save useless effusion of blood, I would
recommend measures be taken for suspension of hostilities and the restoration of peace.[108]

VII. All Is Indeed Lost

On Sunday, April 23, Davis and his Cabinet attended church and heard the Rev. George M. Everhart of St. Peter's Church give a strongly worded sermon about the "passion of madness, crime and outrage." As Davis left the church, he turned to two of his aides and said, "I think the preacher directed his remarks at me; and he really seems to fancy I had something to do with the assassination."[109] Alone in his room that night, Davis heard the cheers of a small group of Confederate soldiers outside his window. He spoke briefly to the men, telling them not to surrender and saying all was not lost.

On Monday, Breckinridge and Reagan arrived in Charlotte with a copy of the treaty with Sherman. Davis called a Cabinet meeting that morning to examine the treaty and found it went far beyond the terms Grant had given Lee. The treaty called for the Confederates to lay down their arms and in exchange they would be welcomed back into the Union with all constitutional rights. Even though Sherman's offer was more lenient than Grant's, it presented new problems for Davis. The treaty Grant offered Lee had been a military document, Sherman was offering a political document, which called for the end of the Confederacy. Davis did not want to be the one to approve the death of his nation.

He hesitated, but the generals and other Cabinet members clearly wanted to accept. Davis was thinking of posterity; he did not want future generations to believe that he had surrendered the Confederacy when there was still a chance of victory. He did not want history to record that if he had just held out a little longer, victory might have been his. So, he asked the members of the Cabinet to write their views on a piece of paper.

Reagan wrote first, laying out clearly the hopeless situation, pointing to the loss of ordnance and munitions and military stores, the fall of workshops and depots, the inadequacy of the army west of the Mississippi and the closing of the ports, the collapse of the Confederate dollar and the hostility among the citizens to the draft: "The country is worn down by a brilliant and heroic, but exhausting and bloody struggle of four years."

Then it was Breckinridge's turn.

> ...The principal army of the Confederacy was recently lost in Virginia. Considerable bodies of troops not attached to that army have either dispersed or marched toward their homes, accompanied by many of their officers. Five days ago the effective force in infantry and artillery of General Johnston's army was by 14,770 men, and it continues to diminish. That officer thinks it wholly impossible for him to make any head against the overwhelming forces of the enemy. Our ports are closed and the sources of foreign supply lost to us. The enemy occupy all of the greater parts of Missouri, Kentucky, Tennessee, Virginia and North Carolina, and move almost at will through the other States to the

> east of the Mississippi. They have recently taken Selma,
> Montgomery, Columbus, Macon and other important
> towns, depriving us of large depots of supplies and of
> munitions of war.... I do not think it would be pos-
> sible to assemble, equip and maintain an army of 30,000
> men at any point east of the Mississippi.... For these,
> and for other reasons which need not now be stated,
> I think we can no longer contend with a reasonable
> hope of success.[110]

Reluctantly, Davis signed the surrender papers, but soon, word came from Johnston that the new administration in Washington had rejected the terms Sherman had offered. President Andrew Johnson, acting under the advice of Secretary of War Edwin Stanton, found Sherman's terms to be entirely too lenient. Johnston must either accept the same terms Lee had agreed to or resume fighting. Johnston knew he could not continue the fight and quickly agreed to the new terms without even bothering to ask Davis.

Davis said he was not surprised at the rejection of the terms, but he was angry with Johnston. After the rejection of the terms, he ordered Johnston to fall back with what men he could and attempt to regroup for another fight. Johnston had completely ignored the order, instead telling his men to lay down their arms and had said the surrender was the result of "recent events in Virginia for breaking every hope of success by war."[111] Lee had fought until he was completely surrounded and a breakout attempt had failed. Johnston had surrendered without making a final stand or attempting a getaway. Davis was also angry because Johnston had not only surrendered his men, but also the Confederate troops in South Carolina and Georgia, men Davis hoped to call upon in his escape to Texas.

In Abbeville, Mrs. Davis used a piece of cheap, black-bordered stationery to write her husband.

Your very sweet letter reached me safely by Mr.
Harrison and was a great relief — I leave here in the
morning at six o'clock for the wagon train going to
Georgia — Washington will be the first point I shall
'unload' at — from there we shall probably go on to
Atlanta, or thereabouts — and wait a little until we hear
something of you — Let me now beseech you not to
calculate upon seeing me unless I happen to cross your
shortest path toward your bourne, be that what it may —
It is surely not the fate to which you invited me in
brighter days, but you must remember that you did not
invite me to a great Hero's home, but to that of a plain
farmer, I have shared all your triumphs, been the only
beneficiary of them, now I am but claiming the privi-
lege for the first time of being all to you now these
pleasures have past for me — My plans are these, subject
to your approval. I think I shall be able to procure
funds enough to enable me to put the two eldest to
school — I shall go to Florida if possible, and from
thence go over to Bermuda, or Nassau, from thence to
England, unless a good school offers elsewhere, and put
them to the best school I can find, and then with the
two youngest join you in Texas — and that is the prospect which bears me up, to be once more with you —
once more to suffer with you if need be — but God loves
those who obey him, and I know there is a future for
you — This people are a craven set, they cannot bear the
tug of War — Here they are all your friends, have the
most unbounded confidence in you. Mr. Burt and his
wife have urged me to live with them — offered to take
the chances of the Yankees with us — begged to have
little Maggie — done everything in fact that relatives
could do — I shall never forget all their generous devotion to you — I have seen a great many men who have
gone through — not one has talked fight. A stand cannot
be made in this country, but do not be induced to try
it — As to the trans-Mississippi, I doubt if at first things
will be straight, but the spirit is there, and the daily
accretions will be great when the deluded of this side

are crushed out between the upper and nether millstone...."[112]

Davis had dispatched Burton Harrison to see Mrs. Davis to safety. Major Armistead Burt had offered to let Mrs. Davis remain at his home, despite her fears that the Yankees would burn the house if they found her there. "I can think of no better use of it," Burt told her.[113]

But Mrs. Davis did not want to stay in Abbeville. She had heard a number of horror stories about the way women had been treated by Sherman's men, and she was anxious to flee. Harrison disagreed. He thought that by fleeing south, and camping beside the roads, the small band would be an even greater target for marauders. Harrison urged her to stay in Abbeville: at worst, she would be captured by Union forces that would insure her safety. But she was adamant.

Their original plan was to go to Atlanta. But when they reached the Savannah River, they learned that smallpox had broken out in the area, and Mrs. Davis was terrified that her children might contract it. A plantation owner heard of her concern and vaccinated her children.

Throughout the journey, she had been plagued by some of the same problems her husband had experienced. In some towns, she was treated with the greatest respect; in others, all but ignored. She wrote,

> The price for provisions on the road, from the hostelries and even the private houses was fifty cents or one dollar for a biscuit, and the same for a glass of milk. It was difficult to feed my children except when we reached the house of some devoted Confederate, and then I did not like to avail of their generosity.

On April 22, A.A. Franklin wrote to Mrs. Davis from Cokesbury Depot, South Carolina.

> I presume you have heard the rumors of yester-
> day, viz, that an armistice of sixty days has been agreed
> upon, the General Grant has sent couriers to the dif-
> ferent raiding parties to that effect; that commissioners
> to negotiate terms had been appointed ... also that the
> French fleet had attacked the Yankee gun boats at New
> Orleans and had taken the city."

On Wednesday, April 26, Davis called another meeting of the Cabinet. The previous meetings had been held in
the director's room of Dewey's branch of the Bank of North
Carolina on South Tryon Street, but this meeting was held in
William Phifer's home on North Tryon, where Trenholm was
recovering from his illness. They discussed plans for their
escape to Texas, and George Davis submitted his resignation,
telling Davis he wanted to stay awhile in Charlotte to care for
his motherless children and then attempt to flee.

It was time for Davis and his five remaining Cabinet
members to move on. Once again the supplies were loaded
into the wagons and the Confederate government was in
flight again.

With the surrender of Johnston, the Union forces east
of the Mississippi could now turn their full attention to capturing Davis. Union Secretary of War Stanton sent telegrams
to federal commanders telling them to capture "the rebel
chiefs." Stanton said the Davis party was carrying $13 million
in gold, which he described as plunder, and told the
commanders that the gold would go to the men capturing
Davis. Brigadier General W.J. Palmer was placed in charge
of the hunt for Davis and commanded to follow him to the
"ends of the earth."[115]

A pattern was now emerging to Davis' travels. As he
went through areas affected by the war, or under threat, he
received inhospitable treatment, but in areas where the war
had not come, he was received as a hero. As he crossed the

state line into South Carolina, he found the stately homes still standing and life much as it had been before the war. As his party moved through the small towns, crowds lined the streets to cheer. In Charlotte, Davis had remarked to Harrison, "I cannot feel like a beaten man."[116]

Davis' guard had increased dramatically in size in Charlotte, and he could now claim the largest army east of the Mississippi. General Echols had been moving north to join Lee near Richmond when he received the news that Lee had surrendered. He offered his troops the choice of surrendering or fighting on. The infantry and half the cavalry chose to go home, and fewer than 1,000 men followed Echols to Charlotte to join Davis. Most of the men rode mules, a mighty comedown for the once proud cavalry.

Davis pushed to Fort Mill the first day, a distance of only seventeen miles. He had planned to go farther, but he encountered a waiting crowd throwing flowers in his path and insisting that he spend the night. Davis and some members stayed at the home of Colonel A.B. Springs, while others stayed with Colonel William E. White.

Fort Mill was the end of the road for Trenholm, whose health continued to be fragile. He had given his all for the Confederacy, and now back in his home state, he wanted only to return to his estate *DeGreffin* near Columbia and try to put his life back together. Postmaster Reagan was named to assume the treasury post. It was strange that Davis would go through the formality of naming Reagan, who previously had no post office to run and now had no treasury to administer.

Before leaving Fort Mill, Davis assembled his remaining Cabinet members on the front lawn of the Springs' home for a meeting. Once again, the topic for discussion was their escape. The cavalry unit accompanying Davis was becoming increasingly disappointed with the slow movement of Davis. They were used to quick movements and trudging behind a wagon did not fit their idea of war. After the meeting, Davis left for Yorkville (now York), about twenty miles away. They had planned to cross the Catawba River over a railroad bridge, but found that the bridge had been burned and had to use the ferry at Nation Ford.

The reception in Yorkville astounded Davis, it was even more enthusiastic than the welcome in Fort Mill. He told aides he had not seen anything like it since 1861 when he arrived in Richmond. He spent the night in the home of James Rufus Bratton.

Despite the reception of Davis, General Duke, the leader of the cavalry, was becoming frustrated, saying at one point that except for Breckinridge nobody "knew what was going on, what was going to be done, or what ought to be done."[117]

On April 30, Davis moved to Unionville (now Union) and stopped for lunch at the home of Brigadier General William H. Wallace, who had not yet returned from the front. They spent the night near Unionville at the home of Mrs. J.R. Giles. The night of May 1 was spent at the home of the mother of General Martin Witherspoon Gary at Cokesbury.

The Confederate treasure was now in Augusta, Georgia, where its chief guard, Captain Parker, was becoming increasingly concerned about its safety. Other military officials in Augusta refused to have anything to do with the treasury. Parker had received orders from Navy Secretary Mallory to disband his corps of midshipmen. But if he carried out that order, there would be no one to guard the treasury. So, Parker ignored the order and decided the best action would be to return the gold to Davis and let him worry about it. He left Augusta and backtracked to Abbeville, where he stored the treasury in the warehouse in the public square and ordered the midshipmen to stand guard to prevent former

Confederate soldiers from stealing it. Even with the guards, the former Confederates gathered around the warehouse waiting for a chance. On the evening of May 1, Parker decided to take a night off and went to a May Day party. Early the next morning, he was awakened by a guard yelling, "The Yankees are coming."[118] Parker rose immediately and called the entire guard together in the public square. He ordered a train brought forward and had the gold loaded for a trip to Newberry. As the train prepared to pull out, Jefferson Davis and his party suddenly arrived. The President once again found himself in possession of the treasury which could only make him more of a target.

In Abbeville, Davis convened what he called a "council of war," a meeting with his remaining Cabinet members and his military advisors, now led by General Braxton Bragg. The meeting began at four p.m. in a large downstairs parlor in the house where Davis was staying. The room had a large window and the roses were in bloom in the garden. One of those present later wrote of Davis, "He seemed in excellent spirits and humor, and the union of dignity and graceful affability and decision, which made his manner usually so striking was very marked in his reception of us."[119]

It had been Davis' custom throughout the war to open all meetings with a joke or story, and even now, he continued the tradition. Then he began: "It is time that we adopt some definite plan upon which the further prosecution of our struggle shall be conducted. I have summoned you for consultation."

Davis repeated his belief that the Confederacy could somehow be saved, the fight continued. He finished, looked at his military aides and said, "I feel that I ought to do nothing now without the advice of my military chiefs." And then he smiled and no one was quite sure whether he had intended the remark as a joke. President Davis, the man who had frequently ignored the advice of his military commanders, was now saying he would do nothing without their advice.

He continued, "Even if the troops now with me be all that I can for the present rely on, 3,000 brave men are enough for a nucleus around which the whole people will rally when the panic which now afflicts them has passed away." There was a moment of silence; the soldiers knew what had to be said. They would not be intimidated by Davis, and yet, none wanted to be the first to speak. Finally, one started and the others joined in. The people were exhausted, further fighting would be senseless cruelty. The generals said the men would not fight on for the Confederacy. One said that to continue the war "would be a cruel injustice to the people of the south. We would be compelled to live on a country already impoverished and would invite its further devastation. We urged that we would be doing a wrong to our men if we persuaded them to such a course; for if they persisted in a conflict so hopeless they would be treated as brigands, and would forfeit all chance of returning to their homes."

Now Davis thought he had a trump card to play. If the generals were right, he said in a rising voice, then why were nearly three thousand men sticking by him? But the generals had their answer ready. "We answered that we were desirous of affording him an opportunity of escaping the degradation of capture, and perhaps a fate which would be direr to the people than even to himself, in still more embittering the feeling between the north and south. We said that we would ask our men to follow us until his safety was assured, and would risk them in battle for that purpose, but would not fire another shot in an effort to continue hostilities."

Davis was overcome, he began to shake and turn pale. The troops would aid him to safety, but would not follow him into battle. He did not speak for several minutes, then said bitterly, "all is indeed lost."[120]

VIII. President and Mrs. Davis Are Captured in Georgia

Davis tried to stand, but his strength had deserted his legs and Breckinridge took a firm hold of his hand. Davis regained his balance and walked out of the room alone. In the parlor, Benjamin began throwing government papers into a roaring fire. Outside, Mallory sought out Davis and submitted his resignation. He told Davis "of the dependent condition of a helpless family,"[121] and said he wanted to go home to Georgia to see his family, then move through Florida and escape.

Reagan joined in the discussion and suggested that Davis disguise himself as an ordinary soldier, find a boat in Florida and sail for Texas. Davis would have none of it. He would not discuss leaving Confederate soil.

Captain Parker had earlier ignored Mallory's order to disband his midshipmen who were guarding the gold, but now that Mallory was leaving, Parker called the young men together and said, "You are hereby detached from the Naval School and leave is granted you to visit your home." Reagan, the Acting Secretary of the Treasury, approved $40 in gold for each midshipman. Some were still uncertain about leaving and one asked Mallory what he should do. "My young friend, I advise you to return to your home in Richmond by the nearest available route."

Davis was not consulted about the order to disband the midshipmen and when he saw one of the boys preparing to leave, told him, "I am very sorry Mr. Mallory gave you that order."[122] The midshipmen were now gone, and the reliability of the cavalry was coming into question. In the streets of Abbeville, many soldiers could be seen selling their weapons and even their uniforms as souvenirs to people who had been removed from the battles. The generals denied it, but no one else doubted that the cavalry was more interested in the gold than the fate of Davis or the Confederacy.

Davis and his shrinking party left Abbeville at eleven p.m. on May 2 and rode through the night to arrive in Washington, Georgia, at ten the next morning. In Washington, Davis found that his wife had left behind a note:

> I dread the Yankees getting news of you so much, you are the country's only hope, and the very best intentioned do not calculate upon a stand this side of the [Mississippi] river. Why not cut loose from your escort? Go swiftly and alone, with the exception of two or three.... May God keep you, my old and only love.[123]

The note served to reinforce what Davis was already thinking: release the cavalrymen who had joined him in Charlotte. He would keep only an escort of Kentucky horsemen, he told Breckinridge, but then he quickly changed his mind. He told Breckinridge to lead five brigades of cavalry as a decoy to attract the federal patrols. He would not take the

Kentucky cavalry, because he said they were "not strong enough to fight and too large to pass without observation."[124]

It was now time to divide up what remained of the Confederate treasure. Breckinridge paid out $108,000 to the cavalry, $26.25 per man. Nearly $230,000 was turned over to the bank officials representing the Richmond banks. Another $86,000 was concealed in the false bottom of a carriage and moved to Charleston, there to be shipped to England and drawn upon when the Confederate government reached Texas. Davis would take $30,000 in gold to cover the expenses of the journey.

When Lee's men surrendered, they received no gold, Johnston's men each received $1.15 and the leavetakers of Davis were paid $26.25 in gold.

The Cabinet was down to three men, Reagan, Breckinridge and Benjamin, and now Benjamin was ready to leave. Unlike many Southern leaders, Benjamin did not have friends in the North to help him if he should be captured. He was also one of the South's most recognizable men and one of the most hated. In fairness, he had given everything he had, but it was time to move on. He might have stayed with Davis, but he knew that the President's indecision would certainly lead to his capture. Davis continued to act like a president, not a fugitive.

Benjamin and Davis spoke alone for several minutes. Benjamin told him, "I could not bear the fatigue of riding as you do, and as I can serve our people no more just now, will you consent to my making an effort to escape through Florida? If you should be in a condition to require me again, I will answer your call at once."[125] Davis said his farewells and the two men parted.

No sooner had Davis made his decision to send the cavalry with Breckinridge than problems developed. the cavalry was ordered to patrol near Washington for Yankee raiders, but the officers were unwilling to do any more fighting and Breckinridge sent a message to Davis:

> I have not heard from you in answer to my note of this day, and the condition of things here, together with great fatigue, have prevented my going forward.
> Nothing can be done with the bulk of this command. It has been with difficulty that anything has been kept in shape. I am having the silver paid to the troops, and will in any event save the gold and have it brought forward in the morning, when I hope Judge Reagan will take it.
> Many of the men have thrown away their arms. Most of them have resolved to remain here under [General John C.] Vaughn and [General George] Dibbrell, and will make terms. A few hundred men will move on and may be depended on for the object we spoke of yesterday.... Out of nearly four thousand men present but a few hundred could be relied on, and they were intermixed with the mass. Threats have just reached me to seize the whole amount, but I hope the guard at hand will be sufficient.[126]

Each man already had his $26.25 and two choices; he could stay and fight, perhaps being killed in a war that had already ended, or go home with his money. They chose to go home. Breckinridge rode off with several hundred men to create a diversion to aid Davis' escape. Ten men were picked to accompany Davis, along with several drivers. Before leaving Washington, Davis held a final meeting with his aides in the bank building. There the President performed his last official act, naming Captain M.H. Clark as acting treasurer. The Confederacy might not have a treasury, but it now had an acting treasury secretary — Reagan — and an acting treasurer.

Before Davis arrived in Washington, Mrs. Davis had spent two nights in the town, resting comfortably in a large house. She wrote,

President and Mrs. Davis Are Captured

> We found the whole town in a state of most
> depressing disorder. General [Arnold] and Mrs. Elzey
> called to see me, and said that when the news of the sur-
> render was received there, the quartermasters' and com-
> missaries' stores had been sacked. I was anxious to get
> off before Mr. Davis could reach Washington, fearful
> that his uneasiness about our safety would cause him to
> keep near our train and of his being pursued by the
> enemy.[127]

Mrs. Davis wanted to leave Washington, but she told
Harrison that she had no money. Judge William Crump, an
assistant treasury secretary, had been sent to Washington during
the evacuation of Richmond with a small amount of money,
which he placed in the vault of a Washington bank. Harrison,
who like Mrs. Davis did not have a cent, went to Crump and
asked for some of the money. He awoke Crump in the middle
of the night and found him in a disagreeable mood, telling
Harrison he had no authority to give Mrs. Davis any gold.
The two argued and finally he agreed to give Mrs. Davis
several hundred dollars in gold and Harrison $110.

The following day as Mrs. Davis prepared to leave,
Harrison met two officers, one from Mississippi, the other
from Louisiana, returning from furloughs. One of the men
loaned Mrs. Davis a covered wagon and both agreed to
accompany her. That night she camped in a pine grove and
was preparing to retire for the night when they learned that
some men were planning to raid their camp during the night
and steal their mules and wagons. Harrison met with the
handful of guards and decided to confront the marauders,
knowing that there was no way they could defend their camp
against superior numbers. They told the marauders that Mrs.
Davis was in their party and they were fleeing Union patrols.
The leader of the men immediately went to Mrs. Davis and
apologized, saying he thought the party contained stolen

wagons and supplies and they figured they had as much right as anyone to the supplies.

In Washington, Davis ordered thousands of state papers destroyed, but some of the papers Davis wanted to save, along with his message books and letters, were sewn into blankets and hidden in the home of Mrs. Henry Leovy.

In his final meeting with his aides, Davis once again spoke of escaping to the West and starting over again. It was never clear whether Davis dreamed of organizing a new Confederacy, consisting of Texas, Arkansas, Missouri, Arizona, New Mexico and what is now Oklahoma, or using it as a base to retake the Confederate states east of the Mississippi. Increasingly, Davis was advised that the land journey to Texas was impossible. Union troops had a firm hold on Georgia, Alabama and Mississippi, and the only chance for escape was to make for the east coast of Florida, sail around the peninsula, into the Gulf of Mexico and on to Texas. Colonel Charles Thorburn, a former naval officer, was placed in charge of mapping an escape for Davis by sea. He had hidden a small boat on the Indian River in Florida to be used in the escape.

Anticipating this, Sherman had dispatched an aide to Key West, Florida, with instructions to place extra patrols along the Florida coast to look for Davis.

Before leaving Washington, Davis again wrote his wife explaining his decision to disband his cavalry guard. He had wanted them, but said,

> They have become so much demoralized ... that I can no longer rely on them in case we should encounter the enemy. I have therefore determined to disband them and try to make my escape, as a small body of men elude the vigilance of the enemy easier than a large number. They will make every effort in their power to capture me and it behooves us to face these dangers.... We will go to Mississippi, and there

rely on [General Nathan Bedford] Forrest, if he is in
a state of organization, and it is hoped that he is; if
not, we will cross the Mississippi River and join Kirby
Smith, where we can carry on the war forever.[128]

President Davis' plan of re-establishing the Confederacy west of the Mississippi may have seemed like folly, but for him it held real possibilities. Smith had some 40,000 men who had not endured the defeat and deprivations that the troops east of the Mississippi had suffered for the past four years. There was other support in the West; the Confederacy had signed treaties with Indian tribes during the war and Davis counted on them for help. Finally, the area in the West had no large cities to defend, it could take the Union troops years to track down the Confederate troops. But there was one major flaw with Davis' theory. The reason Smith's army was intact was that the Union troops had been preoccupied with the fighting east of the Mississippi. Smith's men had seen little combat and their usefulness would be questionable against battle-hardened Union troops.

Now, Davis and his small party set off again, this time with just one wagon and two ambulances. On May 6, the Davis party arrived in Sandersville, Georgia, and there decided to break into two groups. Clark, the acting treasurer, would take some of the guards and ride on to Florida to prepare for the arrival of Davis. The President said he would join them in Madison or Tallahassee. Now, Davis had only a handful of soldiers, Reagan, Captain Campbell and four aides. They were close to the Florida border and the safety of the swamps and overgrown brush.

Union forces stepped up their efforts to find Davis. On March 5, General Palmer arrived in Athens, Georgia, after a forced march. His information was wrong, Davis was not en route to Athens, but Palmer sent his men to search the area.

Davis was increasingly worried about the safety of his wife, who had been traveling about a day ahead of his party since leaving Abbeville. She worried that her presence would slow her husband and lead to his capture, but Davis knew that the area was infested with disorganized soldiery — both Union and Confederate — and if they found Mrs. Davis they might assume she had the Confederate treasury. And he was also afraid he might be forced to flee the country and leave his wife behind.

After traveling at a slow pace for more than a month, Davis quickened his speed on May 8. After a hard ride, he came within 100 miles of the Florida border. But Captain Campbell told Davis that the horses and men were exhausted and could go no further that night. As Davis and his aides prepared to make camp, Colonel Preston Johnston strolled down to the ferry crossing they would be using the following morning, and learned that Mrs. Davis and the children had passed through that morning. He also heard that a group of former Confederate soldiers knew of the presence of Mrs. Davis and planned to attack her camp. Johnston immediately returned and told Davis.

The President remounted his horse, telling his men. "I do not feel that you are bound to go with me, but I must protect my family."[129] Some of his aides and guards decided to make the trip, despite the exhaustion and they rode hard for nearly twenty miles. Some of the men were forced to drop behind as their horses collapsed, but Davis and some others with better mounts were able to continue. Near Dublin, Georgia, they spotted a small camp off the road and as they approached, a voice yelled out, "Who comes there?"[130] Davis recognized the voice immediately as that of his aide, Burton Harrison, who had been escorting Mrs. Davis.

Davis found the camp prepared for an attack, the wagons circled and soldiers sleeping near their guns, ready to

94

spring into action. Mrs. Davis was overjoyed to see her husband, but at once urged him to leave, before he jeopardized his own safety. But Davis was tired and did not want to continue that night. He told her he would see her through for a day or two, then leave on his own.

On the morning of May 9, they moved south, with Davis and his wife riding in an ambulance. Their son Jeff, too young to realize the seriousness of the situation, jumped around crying out for attention. To keep him quiet, Davis showed his son how to shoot a derringer at a target. On the night of May 9, they stopped near the town of Irwinsville just sixty-five miles from the Florida border. Davis went to sleep quickly, not even bothering to remove his gray frock coat and trousers. His aides were equally weary and somewhat discouraged by the slow progress they were making. But they realized they were closing in on the Florida border, where it would be nearly impossible for them to be captured. The President's horse was kept saddled in case of trouble.

In the early morning hours, his guards began to doze off, the pace of the past days overcoming them at last. Two regiments of Union cavalry, the 4th Michigan and the 1st Wisconsin, had been searching for Davis. At Hawkinsville, Georgia, they learned that Davis was in the area and intensified their search. At dawn, the two units approached the Davis camp, one from the south, the other from the northwest.

At daybreak on May 10, the free Negro servant James Jones was awakened by the sound of horses, and he rushed to John Taylor Wood and Colonel Johnston.

Johnston told Jones to arouse Davis, his first thought being that a marauding band was near. As Jones awoke Davis, gunfire opened around the camp and horses came pounding toward them. The two units approaching from opposite directions had opened fire on each other, the bullets whizzing around the Davis camp. For fifteen minutes, the shooting continued, leaving two Union soldiers dead and four wounded.

Davis, still in his tent, quickly looked out the flap of his tent and yelled to his wife, "Those men have attacked us at last." He assumed they were marauders after the treasure. "I will go out and see if I cannot stop the firing; surely I will have some authority with the Confederates." But he soon realized that the men were Union troopers and said to his wife, "The Federal cavalry are upon us."[131]

A Union officer rode into the camp and shouted at Harrison, "Have you any men with you?" Harrison quickly replied. "Of course we have, don't you hear them firing?"[132] Davis watched the action for less than a minute, then grabbed a raglan cloak and ran out of his tent toward his saddled horse. By mistake, he had grabbed his wife's cloak, a mistake that would haunt him for the rest of his life. As he grabbed the reins of his horse to mount, a Union soldier screamed, "Halt." Davis turned to face the soldier and found he was looking down the barrel of a carbine, Davis would later write that "I expected, if he fired, he would miss me, and my intention was in that event to put my hand under his foot, tumble him off the other side (of his horse), spring into the saddle and attempt to escape."[133]

But Mrs. Davis had been watching and fearing that her husband might try something bold, although foolish, rushed to him and threw her arms around him. Ironically, Davis, for whom the entire escape had been planned, was the first major official of the Confederacy to be captured.

Colonel B.D. Pritchard, commander of the Union troops, soon realized that the shooting was his own men firing on each other in the confusion and began shouting for the firing to be halted. Not a single Confederate shot was fired in the capture. Pritchard rode up to Davis and smiled, saying,

"Well, old Jeff, we've got you at last." At this, Davis lost his temper and shouted, "The worst of all is that I should be captured by a band of thieves and scoundrels."[134]

Pritchard lost his smile and said, "You're a prisoner and can afford to talk that way."[135]

In the confusion, John Taylor Wood slipped a $20 gold piece to one of the Union soldiers and made his escape. In another part of the camp, Colonel Lubbock was struggling with two soldiers who wanted his saddlebags. One Union trooper told Lubbock they would kill him if he did not surrender the bags, "Shoot and be dammed, but you'll not rob me while I'm alive and looking on," Lubbock snapped.

The soldiers wrested the bag from Lubbock and he walked over to Davis and said, "This is bad business."[136] Unlike Lubbock, Reagan quickly surrendered his saddlebags with $3,500 in gold. Suddenly a shot rang out and the Union troopers thought that the Confederate gold had been found. But is was only an overanxious Yankee using his rifle butt to break open a trunk. He did not find any gold, but when the gun fired, he blew his hand off.

Union soldiers quickly gathered around the trunk and ignoring their wounded comrade started to rifle through its contents. They found only some of Mrs. Davis' clothes, but they would turn out to have value to the Union.

As the Union officers went through his wife's clothing and some of the men ate food intended for his children, Davis snapped, "You are expert set of thieves." One of the men looked up from his food and said, "Think so?"

Davis turned to Reagan and in a low voice said, "God's will be done," and he walked to take a seat on a fallen tree beside the campfire.

Three days later, General James Wilson informed the War Department that in trying to escape, Davis, "Hastily put on one of Mrs. Davis' dresses and started for the woods, closely pursued by our men, who at first thought him a woman, but seeing his boots while running, suspected his sex at once. The race was a short one, and the rebel president soon was brought to bay. He brandished a knife of elegant pattern, and showed signs of battle, but yielded promptly to the persuasion of Colt revolvers without compelling our men to fire."

The story quickly spread throughout the north. In later years it was difficult to tell which bothered Davis more, his capture or the stories that he tried to escape in his wife's clothes.

They left immediately for Macon and along the way his Union guards taunted Davis, saying, "Get a move, Jeff." As the Union unit passed Confederate soldiers returning home the Yankees would sing out, "Hey, Johnny Reb, we've got your President." At last, a Confederate soldier shouted back, "Yes, and the devil's got yours."

As they traveled, Davis learned for the first time that President Johnson had issued a proclamation charging Davis with complicity in Lincoln's assassination. He listened to the news quietly, then said that there was one man who surely knew that he had no involvement in Lincoln's death: "The one who signed it for he [Johnson] at least knew that I preferred Lincoln to himself."[137]

The trip to Macon took three days, and on May 13 they finally arrived. Davis was taken to a hotel where the Union troops had established a headquarters. Davis and his family were given a large, comfortable room and after dinner he met with General Wilson. Davis asked if Wilson would allow him to be taken north by boat. He explained that the overland journey of the previous five weeks had been very difficult for his wife and children and he did not want them to go through it again. Wilson agreed.

The following morning, Davis and his wife were

98

placed on a prison train and taken to Augusta, Georgia. Davis and his wife were placed on a boat for the trip to Savannah. Davis was surprised to see his vice president, Alexander Stephens, who was also on his way to prison. It might have seemed strange to Stephens, a long-time enemy of Davis' and one who had even taken part in talks to end the war, to find himself bound for prison with Davis. Stephens, a child-sized man, was once described as "an advance agent of a famine" because of his appearance. He wore a coat several sizes too large and several mufflers, even though the weather was warm. Davis looked at Stephens, gave a long formal bow, then moved on.

A tug boat loaded with people made its way near the ship that would take Davis to Savannah. Davis stood on the deck as the people began to jeer and taunt him. Davis turned away and looked at an axe hanging on the wall. A union soldier saw Davis and worried that he might try to grab the axe. Quickly, the axe was removed.

On Friday, May 12, Davis was on his way to a solitary cell at Fortress Monroe while in Texas, where Davis had hoped to re-establish his government, the last battle of the Civil War was taking place. Near Brownsville, Union and Confederate forces clashed in a minor battle. History would record that the final battle of the war was won by the Confederate forces.

On the morning of May 16, Davis was transferred to the ocean steamer *William P. Clyde* for the journey to a cell at Fortress Monroe.

When Davis was captured, Captain Clark and his small group of men were en route to Florida to make arrangements for Davis' escape. Their journey was dull, and to pass the time they invented a game. Clark announced that he planned to write a book about the exploits and asked the men to contribute suggestions. From time to time, someone would suggest an entry and the others would debate its merits. They were cut off from the outside world and it was not until May 18, as they approached Gainesville, that they heard that Davis had been captured. They dismissed the information as a rumor and pushed on to Gainesville.

Four days later they received confirmation of Davis' arrest and Clark proposed that the papers and baggage be left at a home near Gainesville. Clark told the men that under the authority granted him by Reagan, he could pay the members of the party some of the gold he carried, and take the balance to England to await further instructions from Davis or Reagan. He proposed that the gold be used to hire lawyers to defend Davis.

Clark's plan drew nothing but opposition from the other members of the party. Watson Van Benthuysen and his brothers claimed that the gold was in their care, since Van Benthuysen had been named quartermaster. He suggested that it be divided with three quarters going to members of the party and the remainder going to Mrs. Davis. Then, he added that since he was a distant relative of Mrs. Davis, he should hold her share.

Clark was outnumbered and agreed to the distribution, but stipulated that everyone sign a receipt for the money. Watson Van Benthuysen took $6,790 and the eight other members of the party each got $1,940. Five Negro servants received twenty dollars each and Davis' personal cook and guard were paid $250 apiece. Clark returned to Abbeville to sort through some of the papers Davis left behind in the flight south. Acting under previous orders, he destroyed many of the papers, including records of promotions, exemptions and appointments, but he retained all letters from generals, governors and members of the Cabinet. Once again, he hid the papers and returned home.

The Van Benthuysen brothers returned to their homes

in Baltimore with their gold. Later, when Davis wrote Watson Van Benthuysen asking for the money to underwrite his defense, he was sent just $1,500.

In Washington, D.C., United States war secretary Edwin Stanton learned that some of Davis' belongings had been left in Gainesville. Hoping to find evidence to link Davis with the assassination of Lincoln, he ordered the Union troops to find the baggage and search for clues. The Yankees were surprised to find the trunk and bags stored in a room near the train station. Inside, they found $20,000 in Confederate money and portraits of Davis, his wife and General Lee. They did find one important set of documents, the letters the Cabinet members had written in Charlotte recommending that General Johnston accept the surrender terms offered by Sherman. The baggage and its contents were taken to Washington, Georgia, where it stayed until 1874, when it was returned to Davis.

IX. Breckinridge and Party Struggle to Cuba

The flight south had been particularly difficult for Breckinridge, who had hoped to bring the war to an end in a dignified manner. The refusal of Davis to admit that the war was lost and the declining loyalty of the Confederate troops troubled him. But he was also very worried about his personal safety. During the peace negotiations with Sherman in North Carolina, the Union General had pulled him aside and warned Breckinridge that Northerners were especially bitter towards him. He had seen evidence of that bitterness in 1863, when Northern newspapers reported that he had been killed in battle and *The New York Times* wrote, "Of all the accursed traitors of the land there has been none more heinously false than he—none whose memory will live in darker ignominy."[138]

On the morning of May 3, Breckinridge was in Georgia attempting to catch up with Davis and his party. He received intelligence reports that Union patrols were in the area, and he hurried to reach Davis. But the soldiers traveling with him were not so anxious; they refused to advance unless they received some of the money they were owed in back wages. The money was paid but precious time had been lost and they arrived in Washington, Georgia, just one hour after Davis had left on the morning of May 4.

Breckinridge briefly considered attempting to catch Davis, but then hesistated. After considering the options he decided that he should start worrying about himself and plan his own escape. He put about $25,000 of Confederate gold into safe hands, keeping $1,000 for himself and disbanded the War Department. He told most of the men traveling with him to return to their homes and, on May 5, he set off with 45 volunteers. Even now, he continued to think about Davis, hoping that his band of 45 men would lure Union patrols away from the President.

By the following morning, Breckinridge had traveled just eleven miles, when he heard that Union troops were approaching. He was outnumbered five to one and he gave orders that a fight should be avoided, dispatching an aide to discuss peace terms with the Union commander. While the two sides talked, Breckinridge escaped, accompanied by his two sons, Cabell, twenty, and Clifton, eighteen; Lieutenant James Clay, Jr., the grandson of Henry Clay; Lieutenant Colonel James Wilson and slave named Tom Ferguson, who belonged to a staff officer.

As soon as Breckinridge was safely away, he sent back instructions for his men to surrender. "I will not have one of these young men to encounter one hazard more for my sake," he said.[139]

Breckinridge now decided that he should not try to rejoin Davis, who was about forty miles away. He decided to disguise himself, trimming his well-known mustache, changing into a black broadcloth suit and adopting an alias,

104

"Colonel Cabell." He then headed south, working his way toward Madison, Florida, an unofficial meeting place for the fleeing Confederates.

He sent his son Clifton and Lieutenant Clay back to Kentucky; the journey would be hard, and there was no reason for them to flee. The following day, Breckinridge rode sixty miles, camping at Jacksonville, Georgia, for the night. As he camped, the Federal patrol captured Davis.

As Davis was escorted under Federal guard to the Georgia coast, Breckinridge lay in the grass contemplating his future. Finally, he pulled a book from his saddlebags and began to read Plutarch's *Decline and Fall of Athens*.

They had expected to met by a boat at the Ocmulgee River, but when they arrived the boat was not there. A scout was sent to look for the boat and it took several hours to find it. The boat was small, and it took several trips to ferry the men across the river and finally, only Breckinridge was left standing on the north side of the river. When the boat returned for him, Wilson called to him several times without response. Wilson noticed that Breckinridge seemed lost in thought and as the boat approached, he heard him reciting the last stanza of the poem, "Oh, Come to the South."[140]

> Oh, here would the beauty brilliantly beam,
> And life pass away like some delicate dream;
> Each wish of thy heart should realized by,
> And this beautiful land seem an Eden to thee.

On May 11, Breckinridge stopped at Milltown, Georgia, just north of the Florida border and decided to wait for Davis, unaware that he was under Federal guard. Breckinridge had been waiting for three days when word finally came that Davis had been captured. Breckinridge crossed into Florida on May 15, arriving in Madison.

At the home of General Joseph Finegan, the Confederate commander for Florida, he met Captain John Taylor Wood, the Davis aide who had escaped capture. Wood decided to join Breckinridge in his flight with Wilson and Ferguson. Breckinridge decided to send his other son, Cabell, home and told him he did not plan on returning to the United States.

Florida had only 140,000 residents, nearly half of them slaves. Most of the people were centered in Pensacola and St. Augustine. The state's primary road connected those two cities. Except for the new capital of Tallahassee and some other scattered villages, there was almost nothing in between.

About twenty-five miles east of Madison, Breckinridge stopped to spend the night at the home of Lewis M. Moseley, and learned that Benjamin had passed through two days earlier, following the same route. Moseley's ferry carried Breckinridge across the Suwannee River on the morning of May 16, and for the first time, they encountered the heat and mosquitoes that would plague their journey, along with a shortage of drinking water.

They passed the night of May 17 at Collins, a stagecoach station near the present city of Live Oak. Accommodations were few and they slept on the floor of a local tavern. Breckinridge and his party arrived in Gainesville on May 18, hoping to stay at the home of former Confederate Congressman James B. Dawkins. But they found that Dawkins already had a house full of visitors and they were forced to sleep at a local tavern that Breckinridge called "a filthy hole."

Early the next morning, they began mapping plans for their escape. Breckinridge told his aides, "It would not do to attempt to leave the country from the West Coast of Florida."[141] He decided that the East Coast would be a better route.

Breckinridge turned to the problem of finding a boat,

since the vessel intended for Davis' escape had been destroyed following the capture of the President. Captain J.J. Dickinson came to the rescue, offering his services. "It was his [Breckinridge's] earnest desire to reach the Trans-Mississippi department and join Generals Kirby Smith and [John] Magruder before they surrendered, and thought the safest route to this objective point would be by way of Cuba, and wished to know if I could arrange to send him at once. The only means of transportation that I could offer was a lifeboat I had captured with the gunboat Columbine on the St. Johns River," Dickinson wrote.[142]

Colonel Wood, also seeking to escape from the Federals, arrived in Gainesville that morning and set off immediately to locate Benjamin and Colonel Thorburn. He was unable to find either and returned to join Breckinridge.

On May 20 Mallory was arrested at LaGrange, Georgia, as he slept.

Breckinridge was now close to Ocala, a small community near the center of the state, relatively safe from Union patrols and he received a warm welcome from the large plantation owners in the area. He was treated to fine meals and even went sightseeing, while Colonel Wood took a swim in a nearby lake.

On May 25, Breckinridge reached Umatilla, a small trading community where he purchased supplies. They were now about to leave civilization behind and enter a deserted area of the state. On May 26, they set off down the St. Johns River. "It was a small, open craft, about 17 or 18 feet long.... I thought it might do for the river, but it seemed a very frail thing to go on the ocean in," Breckinridge wrote.

Before setting off down the river, Breckinridge performed the last act of the Confederacy, promoting a young lieutenant who had been his guide. "You shall be a major, I will make out your commission," Breckinridge told him.

The lieutenant laughed and said, "Well, you see, general, there's a fellow in our regiment that hasn't done nothing and he is a major and a quartermaster, and if it's all the same to you, I would just like to rank him for once."[143] Breckinridge smiled and wrote out a commission making the man a lieutenant colonel.

Joining them at Lake George on the St. Johns River were three former Confederate soldiers who would help them wind their way down the river: Sergeant Joseph O'Toole, Corporal Richard Russell and Private P. Murphy. The three had recently been paroled from the Confederate Army, but now they risked their lives to help Breckinridge.

The seven men crammed into the boat, their weight all but forcing it beneath the water. The wind was some help, but they spend much of their time rowing and as night fell, a heavy rain began to fall, drenching the men and ruining most of the food and gunpowder. They slept in the middle of the river but it was impossible for any of them to lie down, so they slept sitting up. In the morning, they ate a meal of cornmush with rum and water.

The journey was difficult; there were no maps to guide them and they frequently set off into false channels. Breckinridge said of the river, "It abounds in cranes, pelicans and other water fowl and a great number of crocodiles, who sunned themselves on the bank, and slid into the river with a sudden plunge on our approach. Sometimes they would swim across our bow with their black scaly backs just visible, like a gunboat low in the water. I shot one with my pistol and after we got him ashore it required three more balls through the place where his brains should have been, to finish him. We caught some fish in the river and found some sour oranges in a deserted orchard, with which, and some dark and dirty brown sugar, we made a miserable [orangeade]."[144]

They made several attempts to camp on the shore, but

108

were forced to retreat to the middle of the river by the mosquitoes. On May 29, they landed near Cook's Ferry and for the first time in four nights slept in beds. Private Murphy left the party there, but they were joined by another man who had agreed to transport their boat overland to the Indian River. The roads were little more than muddy paths, and they covered just eighteen miles the first day. That night, they camped near the site of what is Cape Canaveral today, and again sleep was impossible as the mosquitoes attacked by the thousands. Even the oxen suffered from the bites, leaving them covered with blood.

On May 31, they reached the Indian River, but their fate was far from secure. Colonel Wood, the grandson of former President Zachary Taylor, was placed in charge of navigating their boat. Because their boat was small, and the ocean rough, they clung to the coast, stopping once to exchange their tobacco with coastal residents for watermelons. Wood noted that the people were so destitute they "hardly had enough rags to cover them." Small leaks had begun to appear and they were forced to stop several times to caulk the holes.

The Indian River water was salty and there were shortages of drinking water. To Breckinridge's surprise, the mosquitoes became worse. "Someone has said that by swinging a bucket around your head, you could fill it. We can get no rest, except by covering every part of one's person except his nostrils. I tie a towel around my hands and wrists; the clothes they will pierce. Insects are so bad here that cattle cannot live," Wood wrote.

On the night of June 2, the rains came again, but the small group had a more serious problem to worry about, they were approaching a Federal guard post at Indian River Inlet, and decided it would be safest to pass at night. "Approaching cautiously with muffled oars, we saw a fire on the bank,

109

which we supposed to be the guard fire. The night was dark, and keeping the middle of the stream, we glided past without challenge," wrote Breckinridge.

Finally, they were able to escape the Indian River. In the morning, they went ashore to find breakfast. They were out of food and dug in the sand both for water and turtle eggs, polishing off their meal with some wild limes. Then, they entered the Atlantic Ocean. "What a relief it is to get out of the swamps and marshes of the Indian River and into the blue waters of the old ocean and the freedom from mosquitoes; what enjoyment for us," Wood wrote.[145]

The following day, June 4, they landed near the site of the present city of Palm Beach, again running low on provisions. Following the coast provided protection from the rough ocean waves, but it made them more likely to be captured by patrolling Federal boats. Breckinridge decided to make a run for the Bahamas, sixty miles away. They took a final swim in the ocean, had a brief prayer service and set sail, but immediately encountered problems. A strong wind struck and they quickly returned to shore and hid behind the sand dunes. But they had been spotted by a steamer and had two choices, flee into the swamps and face starvation or try to bluff the pursuers. They chose to bluff, although Breckinridge argued that flight would be better.

The steamer came within three hundred yards of the shore and dispatched a row boat full of men to come ashore. Three of the escapees, including Breckinridge waited on shore while Wood and two others rowed out to meet the boat. The three displayed some parole papers and pretended to be hunting and fishing. Their bluff worked and the steamer departed. The Federals were gone, but the high winds remained and Breckinridge was forced to abandon his plan to make a dash for the Bahamas and continued along the coast.

On the morning of June 6, they spotted a camp of Seminole Indians along the shore. The men were now in desperate need of food and stopped to ask the Indians for help. (Ironically, the Indians were living on the shore and scrounging for food because Wood's grandfather had led the military expedition which forced them from their homes.) The men smoked a pipe with the Indians and were given some luntee, a mush that Breckinridge found was slightly thicker than a pancake and "ten times as tough."[146] But it was the first time they had eaten for days, except for some turtle eggs. They set sail again, but soon encountered another boat. Fearing again that it might be a Federal vessel, they turned away. Breckinridge soon realized that the other boat was also seeking to avoid Union ships.

He guessed that the men might be Union deserters and noticed that their craft was much more seaworthy than his. So, Breckinridge, a former United States vice president and a presidential candidate, respected general and Confederate secretary of war, became a pirate. He took down the sail and his men gave chase by rowing hard. Wood later wrote, "The stranger stood out to seaward and endeavored to escape, but slowly we overhauled her, and finally a shot caused her sail to drop."[147]

They found three men in the boat, deserters as Breckinridge had guessed. "They were throughly frightened at first, for our appearance was not calculated to impress them favorably. To our questions, they returned evasive answers or were silent, and finally asked by what authority we had overhauled them. We told them that the war was not over as far as we were concerned; that they were both deserters and pirates, the punishment of which was death; but that under the circumstances we would not surrender them to the first cruiser we met, but would take their pistols and exchange boats," Wood wrote.

"To this they seriously objected. They were well armed and although we outnumbered them five to three (not counting the slave Tom), still if they could get the first bead on us the chances were about equal.

"They were desperate and not disposed to surrender their boat without a tussle. The general and I stepped into their boat and ordered the spokesman and leader to go forward. He hesitated a moment, and two revolvers looked at him in the face.

"Suddenly he obeyed our orders. The general said, 'Wilson disarm that man.' The Colonel with pistol in hand told him to hold up his hands. He did so while the Colonel drew from his belt a navy revolver, and a sheath-knife. The other two made no show of resistance, but handed us their arms."[148]

The exchange was made and Breckinridge and his men set off in their larger boat. But they made a major change of plans: instead of sailing for Nassau, they would make for Cuba. Again, they were swarmed by mosquitoes and frequently found themselves stuck on sandbars but they faced another, more serious obstacle. The men needed supplies before sailing for Cuba, and the only place to obtain them was at a former fort that had become an outlaw post near the present site of Miami.

It was home to twenty or thirty men, many of them deserters from both Union and Confederate armies, and far too powerful for Breckinridge and his five men to overpower. "A more motley and villainous-looking crew never trod the deck of one of Captain Kidd's ships," Wood wrote. "A burly villain, towering head and shoulders above his companions, and whose shaggy black head scorned any covering, hailed us in broken English and asked who we were. Wreckers, I replied; that we had left our vessel outside, and come in for water and provisions. He asked where we had left our vessel, and her name, evidently suspicious, which was not surprising, for our appearance was certainly against us.

"After a noisy powwow, we were told to land, that our papers might be examined. I said, no, but if a canoe were sent off, I would let one of our men go on shore and buy what we wanted. I was determined not to trust our boat within a hundred yards of the shore. Finally, a canoe paddled by two Negroes came off, and said no one but the captain would be permitted to land. O'Toole volunteered to go, but the boatman would not take him, evidently having their orders. I told them to tell their chief that we had intended to spend a few pieces of gold with them, but since he would not permit it, we would go elsewhere for supplies."

The canoe carrying the pirates returned to shore and the Breckinridge party headed south. But the pirates returned to shore only to get reinforcements and soon fifteen or twenty men in four or five canoes were closing in fast. Breckinridge and his men prepared for a fight, deciding that they could not outrun the pirates.

"Though outnumbered three-to-one," Wood wrote, "still we were well under cover in our boat, and could take each canoe as it came up. We determined to take all the chances, and to open fire as soon as they came within range. I told Russell to try a shot at some distance ahead of the others. We broke two paddles on one side and hit one man, not a bad beginning. The canoe dropped to the rear at once; the occupants of the others opened fire, but their shooting was wild from the motions of their small crafts. The general tried and missed; Tom thought he could do better than his master, and he made a good line shot, but short. The general advised husbanding our ammunition until they came within easy range. Waiting a little while, Russell and the Colonel fired together and the bowman of the nearest canoe rolled over, nearly upsetting her. They were now evidently convinced that we were in earnest, and, after firing an ineffectual volley, paddled together to hold a council of war. Soon, a single canoe with three men started for us with a white flag. We hove to, and waited for them to approach. When, within hail, I asked what was wanted, a white man standing in the stern, with two Negroes paddling replied:

"'What did you fire on us for? We are friends.'

"Wood replied, 'Friends do not give chase to friends.'

"The other man said, 'We wanted to find out who you are.'

'I told you who we are, and if you are friends, sell us some provisions.'

'Come ashore, and you can get what you want,' the man said."[148]

Finally, both sides agreed that O'Toole would go ashore for two hours to obtain supplies. He returned with the food and the boat headed down to the Florida Keys. At one point they were chased for several hours by a launch, probably a Federal boat, but Wood managed to outdistance the craft.

Florida faded behind them and they were out of danger from Federal patrols, but the weather remained a constant problem. A storm came up, dumping water into the boat and threatening to overturn the craft.

Breckinridge recalled, "The young men with us were lying in the bottom sick. Suddenly, I was aroused by a wave going over me and half filling the boat, which leaned over until the gunwale was under the water. At the same moment, I observed Captain Wood was overboard, and looking around I saw Col. Wilson as stiff as a stanchion holding on like grim death on the rudder and the sail rope. It was his grip on the latter that was about to sink us.

"I knew just enough to shout to him to let go the rope, which he did, and the strain being taken off, the boat finally righted, Captain Wood fortunately caught a rope as he went and had scrambled on board." They went aground on a reef and waited for morning. On June 8, the storm subsided, but the whirl of water was so great, and the boat so small, that Wood had trouble keeping it on course. Again that night, the seas rose high enough to threaten the boat.

"A worse sea Colonel Wood said he had never seen and he was amazed that the little boat lived through, for which we thanked a gracious Savior," Breckinridge wrote.[149]

The following morning, the men were nearly out of water when they spotted a United States merchant ship and asked for water. The men on the merchant ship stared at Breckinridge, but after his long journey, he hardly looked like a former official of the Confederacy, and the men were given food and water.

On June 10, they first spotted Cuba on the horizon, and although they were almost to safety, their condition was very bad. They had slept little during their twenty-six-day flight, the blazing sun had blistered and burned their feet and legs and the churning sea had left them all sick.

The following day, they entered a small port seventy-five miles from Havana. It was Sunday and as they arrived, they heard the ring of church bells. Breckinridge recalled that two months earlier there had been church bells ringing when he left Richmond.

The Confederates may have been hunted criminals in their native country, but in Cuba, they were greeted as heroes. The 13,000 residents of Cardenas gave them a rousing welcome, along with new clothes and good food. The Spanish governor of the island, General Domingo Dulce, sent an escort to bring Breckinridge to Havana. In Havana, they received another welcome and Breckinridge was asked to make Havana his home, but he decided to continue on to England.

Now, it was time for the six men who had been

115

through so much to go their separate ways. Russell and O'Toole returned to Florida and Tom Ferguson, now a free man, went back to Alabama and his family. Captain Wood sailed for Nova Scotia, where he lived for the rest of his life and Colonel Wilson returned to Kentucky and opened a hotel.

Breckinridge sailed for England.

The Evacuation of Richmond, April 1865. Mayo Bridge. Courtesy Valentine Museum, Richmond.

Jefferson Davis, President, Confederate States of America, ca. 1860.
Photograph by Mathew Brady.

Robert E. Lee, General-in-Chief, Confederate Army, ca. 1864.
Photograph by J. Vannerson.

John C. Breckinridge, Secretary of War, C.S.A. Courtesy Library
of Congress.

Judah P. Benjamin, Secretary of State, C.S.A. Courtesy Library of Congress.

George Davis, Attorney General, C.S.A. Courtesy the Museum of
the Confederacy, Richmond.

George Trenholm, Secretary of the Treasury, C.S.A. Courtesy the Museum of the Confederacy, Richmond.

Stephen R. Mallory, Secretary of the Navy, C.S.A. Courtesy
Library of Congress.

John H. Reagan, Postmaster General, C.S.A. Courtesy Library
of Congress.

Richmond after the war. Courtesy Library of Congress.

Above and next two pages: sketches (courtesy Library of Congress) by Illustrated London News artist Frank Vizetelly, who accompanied Jefferson Davis until two days before his capture. This page: flight over the Georgia Ridge.

Above: Jefferson Davis signing acts of government, in flight; opposite Davis bidding farewell to his escort, two days before his capture. Sketches by Frank Vizetelly.

Opposite: satirical cartoon, 1865; Above: Davis' house in Richmond. Courtesy Library of Congress.

The Confederate Capitol, Richmond, after the city fell. Courtesy Library of Congress.

X. Benjamin and George Davis
Go Their Ways

On June 14, as Breckinridge was being feted in Havana, Treasury Secretary Trenholm was arrested near Columbia and held at the city jail in Charleston. After spending several days in jail, he was paroled because of his poor health and his efforts to improve the welfare of the Union prisoners of war. But Union War Secretary Stanton was not in a charitable mood and ordered that Trenholm's property be confiscated and for him to be moved from Charleston and reimprisoned at Fort Pulaski.

Trenholm, Mallory, Reagan and Jefferson Davis were in jail and Breckinridge was safe in Cuba, but there were still two Cabinet members seeking to avoid arrest.

Benjamin had promised Davis that he would rejoin him in Texas, but clearly had no intention of keeping that promise. He was determined to get as far away from the Confederacy as possible. He told Reagan he would keep going, "If

117

it takes me to the middle of China."[150] He wrote to his sister that he preferred to risk death in attempting to escape than endure the "savage cruelty" that he thought would await him if he were captured.

Two days after Davis was captured, Benjamin was spotted by Colonel Wood driving a buggy and accompanied by Colonel H. J. Leovy. Benjamin had disguised himself as a French gentleman, and called himself Monsieur Bonfal. "With goggles on, his beard grown, a hat well over his face, and a large cloak hiding his figure, no one would have recognized him as the late secretary of state of the Confederacy," Wood wrote.[151]

Although the disguise as a Frenchman might have been the most imaginative among several, Benjamin relied mostly on a disguise as a farmer. "I found my most successful disguise to be that of a farmer. I professed to be traveling in Florida in search of land on which to settle, with some friends who desired to move from South Carolina. I got a kind farmer's wife to make me some homespun clothes, just like her husband's. I got my horse the commonest and roughest equipment that I could find."[152]

Benjamin slipped into Florida two days ahead of Breckinridge and decided to follow the same route Breckinridge had laid out. But he was unable to secure a boat and decided to move toward Florida's West coast. He obtained help from loyal Confederates and found refuge at a large plantation on the Manatee River. Soon after he arrived, a Federal scouting party turned up looking for Confederate officials. Benjamin hid in the woods while the Federals searched the house. He again changed his name, this time calling himself Mr. Howard.

Benjamin actually had two problems; fleeing the Confederacy was the more pressing, but he also had to worry about thieves, who would gladly slit his throat for his gold.

118

Near the village of Manatee, he stayed at the home of Captain Frederick Tresca, where Mrs. Tresca sewed the gold into the back of Benjamin's waistcoat. Captain Tresca had been a blockade runner during the war and was familiar with the coastal waterways. He agreed to help Benjamin escape and spent two weeks mapping out their route. The Reverend Ezechiel Glazier, an early supporter of the Confederate cause, agreed to help Benjamin travel to Sarasota Bay, where the city of Sarasota is now located. Tresca met Benjamin there, after securing a small boat and the services of a former Confederate sailor, H.A. McLeod, and they set sail on June 23.

They sailed as far as Gasparilla, where they spotted a Federal patrol boat and quickly hid. "We put in at Gasparilla Pass and as there was no wind, we lowered the mast as soon as we got behind the island, pulled our boat under the mangrove bushes until completely hidden, lay down and waited. The pursuing boat came on, searching diligently, and once came so near that we could hear them talking; but we kept quiet, so quiet indeed, that above the voices of our enemies, and the taunting song of the mosquitoes, against whose attack we were quite helpless, rose the hollow sound of our beating hearts," McLeod wrote.

The Union patrols left and the three men set camp on Gasparilla Island. They remained on the island for two nights, but did not light a fire for fear of being spotted. Near the present city of Naples, they found some bananas to help vary their diet, which had consisted only of fish. Like Breckinridge, Benjamin encountered only a few people in the deserted region, and those they did see were, like Benjamin, running away from something.

At Knights Key, Tresca obtained a larger boat for their trip into the open sea. They sailed for the island of Bimini, a four-day journey, and found the waters rough. "Squalls and

119

water sprouts and tropical storms came near finishing us. The water came down in sheets. I took a tin pan and bailed and Mr. Benjamin used his hat and turning to me said with a smile, 'McLeod this is not like being Secretary of State.'"[153]

As he had on the train from Richmond, Benjamin enlivened the journey with stories and jokes. Benjamin paid Tresca $1,500 in gold for the seventeen-day trip. The threat of capture was over and Benjamin booked passage on a small sloop for Nassau. He quickly suffered another mishap as his ship floundered and sank.

"We had barely time to jump into a small skiff that the sloop had in tow before she went to the bottom. In the skiff, leaky with but a single oar, with no provisions save a pot of rice that had just been cooked for breakfast, and a small keg of water, I found myself at eight o'clock in the morning with three Negroes for my companions in disaster, only five inches of boat out of the water, on the broad ocean, with the certainty that we could not survive five minutes if the sea became the least rough."[154]

The seas remained calm and in the afternoon the men were rescued by a passing ship. They returned Benjamin to Bimini, where he chartered a boat and again set sail for Nassau. The seas were so calm this time it took six days to make the journey. The day after arriving in Nassau, Benjamin left for Havana, where he received a warm welcome. Included in the welcoming party was General Kirby Smith, who had arrived from Mexico after fleeing Texas. Benjamin stayed in Havana briefly, then left for England.

George Davis, the attorney general of the Confederacy, had been the first to resign from the Cabinet, leaving in order to look after his motherless children. He quickly made arrangements for the children and left immediately for Camden, South Carolina, and the home of a relative, the Reverend Thomas Frederick Davis. Like Benjamin, he took another name, calling himself Hugh Thompson. For five weeks, Davis roamed through South Carolina and Georgia with only a horse and carrying his possessions in his saddle bags. In early June, he crossed into Florida and headed south.

On June 3, he reached the plantation of his cousin, Mrs. Thomas Lane, near Lake City. Mrs. Lane did not even tell her husband the true identity of their visitor and after resting for two days, he moved on to another plantation near Gainesville. There he stayed for ten days before moving on to Ocala, where he remained for six days. It was not that Davis was moving slowly because he was afraid, but rather, he hesitated because he was unsure of what to do. Davis had become attorney general only after two other men turned down the position. He had played a minor role in the Davis Cabinet and slowed his travel in an effort to determine what the Union policy would be in dealing with the former Confederate officials. Benjamin was confident there would be a rope waiting for him if he was caught, but George Davis was not sure what awaited him. He was reluctant to leave his home. Unlike Benjamin, he had not saved a large quantity of gold for the trip and unlike Breckinridge, Davis did not have friends to aid him in his escape.

But as he waited, he saw the Federal policy emerging. Jefferson Davis, Stephens, Mallory and Reagan were in jail and the former Confederate states were being treated like conquered territories.

George Davis left Ocala and headed for the remote area of Sumter County to the south. He had now decided to make his escape, but could not obtain help. For three months he went from farm to farm asking for aid. He could not find Benjamin or Breckinridge and had no way of knowing they were already en route to England. He was about to give up when he learned of a boat sailing from the East coast to Nassau. He went to New Smyrna to arrange for passage, but because he had no money, he agreed to work on the ship for his passage.

"When I first saw the craft in which he proposed to make the voyage, I was amazed at the rashness of the undertaking. The gulf stream between Florida and the Bahamas is notoriously the most dangerous navigation on the whole coast; and fancy the attempt to cross it during the equinox in a little boat about twenty feet long and seven feet wide, with rotten sails and a leaky hull. But the gentleman was determined to go, and I wouldn't be left behind ... the calculation was that, with good luck, we could reach Nassau in five or six days," Davis wrote.

The captain was wrong about the length, as Davis soon learned. For thirty-three days they sailed along the coast of Florida, being hit by storms, running aground frequently and often running low on food. Their plight was so bad, they could not even consider setting out across the ocean for Nassau.

On October 18, 1865, Davis landed at Key West after bad weather forced the small boat ashore at the spot where the Union Navy had its greatest strength in the South. There, Davis found that Stephens, Reagan and Trenholm had been released from prison and this encouraged him about his own future. He decided to remain in Key West until he could take a vessel north and surrender to Federal authorities. As he waited for a ship, he was recognized and arrested by federal authorities. He seemed almost relieved to have his ordeal over. "I have no idea what my destination will be ... but if they will let me communicate with and see my friends, even that will be preferable to the life I have been leading."[155]

George Davis was taken to New York and held at Fort Lafayette. He was released on January 1, 1866, and returned to his law practice in Wilmington, never to enter public life again. He died in 1896.

XI. Mallory Languishes in Prison

Jefferson Davis, Trenholm, Mallory and George Davis were in Federal custody. Only two government leaders, Benjamin and Breckinridge, had managed to escape.

Stephen Mallory, along with Benjamin Hill and General Howell Cobb, was taken north from La Grange, Georgia. Mallory said the men traveled by carriage, were given frequent rest periods and were treated with "great civility." Along the way, he wrote to his wife, Angela, telling her to sell their Pensacola home and take the children to Bridgeport. Two days later, on May 27, he wrote again to his wife, saying in part, "I am quite well."[156]

On May 28, Mallory arrived in Chattanooga, where he encountered a Confederate officer who had seen his wife in Atlanta earlier in the week. He questioned the officer about the exact date and realized that he had missed seeing her in Atlanta by just a few hours. That night, he wrote her, "Your affection for me is so sacred ... that ... I feel a pride in you that enables me to bear up bravely...." He again told her to move to Bridgeport. He suggested that she find a "Federal officer who is a gentleman" to act as her escort.

On June 4, Mallory reached Fort Lafayette where he was placed in a cell with Hill. A short time later, they were moved to separate cells. The beds were clean, there were straw mattresses, and the food was plentiful, although plain. His guards allowed him to exercise on the parade grounds, walking alone for more than an hour each day.

He maintained his confidence that he would not be held for a long time. He felt his pre-war service to the Union would put him in good standing for an early release. Several days later, he wrote to Angela again of "the whisperings of a heart from which you are never absent, though I greatly fear that the distance and the obstacles which separate us may permit not an echo of them to reach you."

Mallory, whose political views had always been something of a mystery, now maintained that he had once again become a supporter of the Union. He realized that slavery was dead and wanted only to return home and live quietly.

Again, he wrote another sentimental letter to his wife. "Oh, if I could but see you for an hour! Kiss our little ones for me. Tell my noble boy Buddy that I long ardently to see him. And tell my servants that I count upon their good faith until we meet. God grant that I may be able to do something for them to start them fairly in their new life."

Mallory spent his days quietly, reading books from the fort library and playing chess with himself. He was occasionally allowed to visit with Hill. He was troubled with his health, suffering from frequent bouts of gout and spells of dizziness.

In mid-July, Hill was released from the fort; the news distressed Mallory, who wrote in his diary, "He is gone, and I am here alone. My trust is in God. I rejoiced at his release, but felt my isolation bitterly. God bless him; he will soon embrace his dear wife and children."

Mallory had written to President Andrew Johnson requesting a pardon. He said he was anxious to take the oath of allegiance and to be a good citizen of the United States. He maintained that he had never been disloyal to the Union, believing in his heart that secession was unwise. He told Johnson that he had joined the Confederate Cabinet only at the repeated urgings of Davis. He said that in February, 1862, he had tried to resign his post, but had been turned down.

The failure of Johnson to answer his letter, along with the departure of Hill depressed him. Angela had arrived in Bridgeport in mid-July.

Mallory began working on a new plan to secure his release. He wanted Angela to personally call on Johnson and "in her own frank manner" satisfy the President that his motives in seeking a pardon were sincere.

In August, Federal officials agreed to allow Angela and the children to visit him. He wrote in his diary, "Oh, how glad I was to see her and them! And yet, their presence made me feel so sad that but for an extraordinary exertion to appear cheerful I must have looked down when they left me. I find that in my excitement of mind, I omitted a great many matters which I desired to converse about with Angela."

Fall came, and Mallory was still in prison. In early September, Union War Secretary Stanton came to Fort Lafayette on an inspection tour. He and Mallory sat down across from each other at a small wooden table in Mallory's cell. Stanton listened quietly as Mallory once again made his case for release.

There were other visits from his wife Angela. He wrote in his diary, "Whenever Angela comes, I feel a better man, and am more hopeful of my future, my distant future. She prays for me, and I feel the benefit of them. God give me strength and grace, and self control, never to say an unkind or inconsiderate word to her; for no wife can be more worthy of a husband's devoted affection."

By September 26, his despair was nearly complete. He wrote in his diary, "Never before have I experienced the restlessness and distress that I now feel; and cut off from the counsels of others who might, perhaps, inform me of its cause, I am at a loss to account for these sensations. It is becoming difficult for me to adhere to any line of thought, or to fix my mind upon anything. I sometimes think that this condition of my mind may be the result of my abstinence from meat."

He had still not heard from Johnson, and his wife's appeal to the President had not gone well. He had listened in silence as she urged the release of her husband, but he had made no promise.

At the end of September, Mallory wrote again to Johnson.

> Mr. President, Permit me to throw myself upon your generous kindness. Hearing nothing of my petition to you of the 21 of June last I feared that I failed in the statement of my case.
>
> You are merciful and forbearing; and I am sure you would not inflict one pang upon any human heart but from a high sense of duty. Let me assure you therefore that ... you efforts to raise up the south has my hearty thanks, and I pray you to release me that I may share the benefits they confer upon our people.
>
> If I seem importunate, Mr. President, I implore you to attribute it to my distress. I have been four months a prisoner; I am improverished and ruined; my wife and children, helpless and dependent, are to me a constant source of mental anguish. Her anxiety led her to your presence in my behalf recently, but she had not the power to say to you what filled her heart.
>
> I recognize fully your policy for the restoration

of harmony to a united people, and I will pledge my
good faith to aid it to the extent of my power....

October brought even more bad news for Mallory. His
wife was injured in a train accident and taken back to Bridgeport in serious condition. In addition, the Federal officers had
cut back his exercise periods. And finally, there was a visit
from Postmaster General Reagan, who had been released
from Fort Warren. The two spent two hours talking, and
Reagan then left to return home to Texas.

Another letter came from Angela, who wrote that the
doctors had told her she might not be able to walk for another
two months, as a result of her injuries.

As Christmas came near, Mallory's spirits lagged. On
December 4, he wrote in his diary, "Low spirits and constant
efforts to avoid yielding to them have kept me from recovering
during the past month. If I should yield a single day I fear
that I would lie down and not get up again alive."

Two days later, he wrote in his diary, "Am I to be
released or not? Patience, fortitude, resignation, manhood
befriend me! Suffered much pain for days back, But I must
not complain."

Mallory had little to be optimistic about. Secretary
Stanton continued to urge that Mallory be put on trial for
treason as soon as possible. In January, Angela traveled again
to Washington to plead her husband's cause. She saw President Johnson, who received her politely, but said he could
not grant her request to parole her husband.

But her pleas were having an effect. Stanton was grad-
ually losing his interest in the case and Johnson had never
wanted to bring the case to trial. On March 10, 1866, Mallory
was granted a partial parole and released from Fort Lafayette.

The terms of the parole demanded that Mallory
remain in Bridgeport. Mallory was in dire straits; his law

practice was gone, his house nearly ruined, his health precarious.

In June, Mallory went to Washington to meet with Johnson and Stanton to get permission to return to Florida to rebuild his life. He received permission and moved south. In Richmond, he found rebuilding efforts underway, but decided that the business opportunities for him would be limited. In late June, he arrived in Cedar Hill, Georgia, and then pushed on to Florida.

In Pensacola, he began making repairs to his damaged home. In prison, Mallory had begged for his release, declaring that he had no further interest in public life and only desired to return home to live quietly with his family. But as the months passed, he began to speak out and write his views for the Pensacola newspaper, the *West Florida Commercial*. Increasingly, he railed against what he saw as the "destruction and disruption of the United States Government"[157] by the Supreme Court and the Republican radicals in Congress. By 1869, his writings had reached a fevered pitch. He wrote in the *Commercial* that the "government must be turned back upon its course, and made to resume its original position. If this is not done, and that speedily, the child may be living who will shout, 'Long live the Emperor,' on Pennsylvania Avenue."[158]

His health continued to decline, a combination of troublesome gout and problems with his heart. Early on the morning of November 12, 1873, he died at his home in Pensacola.

XII. Benjamin, Reagan and Trenholm Flourish

For Judah P. Benjamin, the trip to England was a return to his roots. His father had been an unsuccessful fish merchant in Cheapside. Now, Benjamin was returning to England, the unsuccessful official of a failed government.

Despite his public life, Benjamin did everything possible to insure that he remained a man of mystery. To a writer who asked for information on his life, he replied, "I have never kept a diary or retained a copy of a letter written by me. No letter addressed to me by others will be found among my papers when I die." Pierce Butler, Benjamin's biographer said, "he did not leave behind him half a dozen pieces of paper."[159] So secretive was Benjamin that, in the final years of his life, he tried with great success to recover all the letters he had even written. As soon as he had finished reading a letter, he immediately burned it.

Benjamin was born in Saint Thomas in 1811, and grew

up in Charleston. But it may have been an incident which occurred when Benjamin was seventeen that set him on a course to hide his personal background. As a junior at Yale University, Benjamin suddenly left school. His opponents later charged that he was expelled for stealing. Benjamin never commented, except to claim that he had left school because of financial reverses suffered by his father.

But in a letter to Yale President Jeremiah Day, written in 1828, Benjamin wrote, "It is with shame and diffidence that I now address you to solicit your forgiveness and interference with the faculty in my behalf...."[160]

After leaving Yale, Benjamin decided not to return home but to study law in New Orleans. He married a young French Creole and soon became a successful planter and attorney, buying large numbers of slaves to harvest sugar cane.

Benjamin prospered, but his marriage did not. First, there was the difference in their religions. The Catholic bride could never accept her husband's Judaism, and constantly tried to convert him. She also found the life of a planter's wife dull. After about a dozen years of marriage, Natalie Benjamin took their daughter Nanette and moved to Paris.

Now, the great cause ended and the war over, Benjamin arrived in London with a net worth of $20,000 mostly from the sale of cotton he had shipped before the war. His reputation had gone before him. During the war, Benjamin had received wide publicity in British newspapers. A reporter for the *London Times* reporting from Richmond in May, 1861, wrote, "Mr. Benjamin is a short, stout man, with a full face, olive-colored and most decidedly Jewish features, with the brightest large black eyes, one of which is somewhat diverse from the other, and a brisk, lively, agreeable manner, combined with much vivacity of speech and quickness of utterance.... Mr. Benjamin is the most open, frank and cordial of the Confederates whom I have yet met."[161]

Despite his reputation, Benjamin found himself starting over again at the age of fifty-five. His welcome in London was warm; several members of Parliament visited him and he was introduced to Prime Minister Gladstone and his favorite author, Tennyson. But he soon lost nearly all of his money through a bank failure and desperately needed a career. In the United States, Benjamin had twice declined seats on the Supreme Court and was the author of a recognized legal text. But in London, he had to start over as a law student. He quickly passed the bar exam and became one of the nation's leading attorneys.

Throughout his life, he continued to send money to his wife and daughter in Paris, even when he was financially strapped. After he became a successful member of the English bar, he sent his wife $80,000 so she could build a new home in Paris. And he sent his daughter a large dowry when she married a French army officer.

By 1893, Benjamin's health was failing rapidly and he moved to Paris to be cared for by his wife. She nursed him for nearly a year, before he died in 1894.

For nearly three decades, he said nothing of the Confederacy, or his role in the war. Only a handful of letters written by Benjamin survive. By comparison, only one line written by his wife exists. At one point, Benjamin wrote to his wife asking her to hold down expenses. She replied, "Don't talk to me about economy, it is so fatiguing."[162]

As Benjamin lay dying, his wife made her final attempt to bring him into the Catholic church. She had a priest give him the last rites, and he was buried in a Catholic cemetery.

Postmaster General Reagan was taken to Fort Warren in Boston harbor. But his prison term was short, and in October 1865, he was released. Reagan returned to Texas and

131

again became active in politics. He helped write a new constitution for the state and was elected first to the United States House of Representatives and then to the U.S. Senate. He has earned a place in history, not for his role in the Confederacy, but as the father of the Interstate Commerce Commission. Reagan was to live longer than any other Confederate Cabinet member, dying in 1905.

After being held briefly in the city jail at Charleston, Treasury Secretary Trenholm was taken to Fort Pulaski in Savannah. Like Reagan, he was released in October. Soon, he was back in business as a cotton broker and built back some of the fortune he had enjoyed before the war. He returned to the state legislature and played a role in driving out the carpetbagger government that took control of the state following the war. But the war had clearly affected his health and in 1876, at the age of 70, he died.

XIII. Jefferson Davis Is Imprisoned for Two Years

When he was captured in Georgia, Jefferson Davis assumed that he would be taken to Washington, D.C., for trial. But after three days on a rough sea, the steamer *William P. Clyde* dropped anchor at the eastern tip of the York-James peninsula off Virginia. For three days, the ship remained at anchor within sight of Fort Monroe, the giant Union fort with thirty-foot walls that were a hundred feet thick at some points. On May 20, Alexander Stephens and Postmaster General Reagan were removed from the ship and transferred to the warship *Tuscarora* for a trip to Fort Warren in Boston. On May 22, Davis was removed from the ship and taken to shore and the confines of Fort Monroe. As he left the ship, he turned to his wife and said, "Try not to weep, they will gloat over your grief."[163]

Davis then boarded a tug for his trip to shore. At the fort, Davis learned why he had been kept on the ship. The fort's masons had needed the time to turn a subterranean gunroom into a prison cell.

Davis was led to his cell, and left with a single possession, his Bible. At dusk, as he sat reading his Bible, a guard entered his cell accompanied by two burly men Davis thought to be blacksmiths. One of the men carried a length of chain and it quickly became clear to Davis what the men had come for.

"My God," Davis said, "You cannot have been sent to iron me?"

The guard told him he was to be shackled.

"This is too monstrous," said Davis. "I demand, Captain, that you let me see the commanding officer. Can he pretend that such shackles are required to secure the safe custody of a weak old man, so guarded and in such a fort as this?"

Davis shouted, "These are not orders for a soldier, they are orders for a jailor—for a hangman which no soldier wearing a sword should accept. I tell you the world will ring with this disgrace. The war is over; the South is conquered; I have no longer any country but America, and it is for the honor of America, as for my own honor and life, that I plead against this degradation. Kill me! Kill me! Rather than inflict on me and my People through me, this insult worse than death."[164]

But his protests were in vain. The order to the fort's commanding general, Nelson A. Miles came from the War Department, which instructed Miles "to place manacles and fetters upon the hands and feet of Jefferson Davis...."[165]

As one of the blacksmiths approached with the chains, Davis grabbed the man and pushed him across the room. The man raised his hammer and walked toward Davis, but stopped short before he struck Davis. The guard called, and the men held Davis to his cot while the shackles were put on.

The men left the cell and Davis sat up slowly. The heavy chains clanked on the floor and Davis wept.

The shackles stayed on for just five days as the protest mounted. The fort's doctor complained that Davis was not getting any exercise because of the weight of the chains, and civilians in the North said the humiliation was uncalled for.

Dr. John J. Craven, the chief surgeon at the fort, was put in charge of the prisoner's health. In his diary, Craven wrote that when he first visited Davis, he "presented a very miserable and affecting aspect, his eyes restless and fevered, his head shifting from side to side for a cool spot on the pillow. His pulse was full and at ninety, tongue thickly coated, his extremities cold and his head troubled with a long-established neuralgic disorder."[166]

Craven ordered an additional mattress and a new pillow for Davis. These were of some help, but his lack of sleep was primarily caused by the guards. Two guards were assigned to patrol his cell, pacing up and down while Davis tried to sleep. A lamp was kept burning constantly. Every two hours, the guard was changed in a noisy ceremony.

Davis' health was not his first consideration; he was increasingly worried about his wife and children. After Davis was taken from the ship, Mrs. Davis went to his cabin and began to weep. As she cried, two women detectives came in and forced her to strip to her underwear and submit to a search. The soldiers came into the cabin after she had dressed and began going through her clothes, examining them. They took a number of articles with them — mainly the children's clothes. The ship then took her and the family to Savannah. Arriving at the port city, she was unable to find a carriage to take her and the children to a hotel. They walked through the streets in a single file, one faithful servant carrying their luggage.

In Savannah, she was placed under an unusual form of

arrest. Federal guards were assigned to watch her and she was not allowed to leave the city. But she could remain at the hotel and pay her own bills.

Mrs. Davis attempted to communicate with her husband through Dr. Craven. On June 7, Craven received a letter from Varina:

> Shocked by the most terrible newspaper extras issued every afternoon, which represent my husband to be in dying condition, I have taken the liberty of writing you.... Would it trouble you too much to tell me how he sleeps — how his eyes look — are they inflamed? — does he eat anything? — It seems to me that no possible harm could accrue to your government from my knowing my sorrow....
>
> If you are only permitted to say he is well, or he is better, it will be a great comfort to me, who has no other left."[167]

Fort commander Miles refused to allow him to respond to the letter. Despite Miles' hard line, Craven grew more sympathetic with Davis each day. He wrote in his diary on June 9,

> Found Mr. Davis relapsing and very despondent. Complained again of intolerable pains in his head. Was distracted night and day by the unceasing tread of the two sentinels in his room and the gabble of the guards in the outside cell. The arched roof of the casement made it a perfect whispering gallery, in which all sounds were jumbled and repeated.... It was well formed for a torture room of the Inquisition.[168]

But the shackles had touched off a wave of sympathy for Davis in the North, and with each passing day, it grew. He received a letter from a New York attorney, Charles

136

O'Connor, offering to serve as his counsel. But the prison life remained unbearable to the proud man. One afternoon, he awoke from a nap and found that one of his guards had drawn a figure hanging from a rope on his cell wall. He protested, and the drawing was removed.

In Washington, the United States government wrestled with the problem of what to do with Davis. Stanton continued to argue that Davis should be brought to trial, but no one was quite sure what the charge should be. Davis' attorney pressed for a quick trial, feeling that the government's case was weak and would fall apart.

On July 24, the fort commander entered Davis' cell and announced a change of policy; Davis would be allowed to exercise for one hour a day on the fort's ramparts. For the first time in over three months, Davis would be allowed to leave his cell.

In Savannah, Mrs. Davis continued to suffer from worry about her husband and their children. At one point, Federal soldiers bribed four-year-old Willie to sing, "We"ll hang Jeff Davis to a sour apple tree." A Negro trooper aimed his rifle at Davis' son Jeff and threatened to shoot. Two women from Maine threatened to thrash Jeff because of the actions of his father.

As summer wore on, Mrs. Davis decided to send the three oldest children to Canada. In August, Mrs. Davis was allowed to leave Savannah, and moved to the home of George Schley in Mill View, Georgia, about five miles from Augusta.

In October, former President Davis was moved to another cell, this one on the second floor. It was larger and had a fireplace. But the feature he found most attractive was a large screen which allowed him to bathe and go to the bathroom with privacy. On October 11, Davis wrote his wife about his new room. "The dry air, good water and a fire when requisite have already improved my physical condition."[169]

In December, Davis was allowed to have his first visitor, Dr. Charles Minnegerode, the rector of St. Pauls in Richmond. The last time Davis had seen Minnegerode was in April, only hours before he fled Richmond.

The Minnegerode visit cheered Davis, but just two weeks later he received a severe jolt; his friend and physician, John Craven was transferred from the fort. Craven had become a confidant not only to Davis, but also Mrs. Davis. Unfortunately, the commander, Nelson Miles, did not like the relationship, having previously ordered Craven not to speak with the prisoner except to discuss his medical condition.

Miles selected Dr. George Cooper to replace Craven. Miles assumed that Cooper would not become as close to Davis as Craven had, but Miles was to be disappointed.

In February, Dr. Minnegerode visited Davis again and then decided to see War Secretary Stanton to plead for Davis. Stanton agreed to see the minister, but refused to answer any of his questions. Finally, Minnegerode suggested that Davis be allowed to have some privileges, such as freedom of the fort. Stanton exploded, "It makes no difference what the state of the health of Jeff Davis is. His trial will soon come on, no doubt. Time enough till that settles it."[170]

In January, Mrs. Davis was allowed to leave Georgia and traveled to Mississippi. Throughout her journey she received kind attention, the railroads refusing to let her pay for her tickets.

On April 17, 1866, Clement Clay was freed from jail, leaving Davis the only former Confederate official still behind bars. Even the Federal government was beginning to lose faith in its case against Davis. Congress appointed a committee to investigate the case. The War Department turned over all its evidence to Francis Lieber, a respected jurist. Lieber examined the evidence and said, "Davis will not be found guilty and we shall stand there completely beaten."[171]

Nevertheless, in May of 1866, Davis was indicted on a charge of treason by the Circuit Court of the United States in Virginia. The news did not come as a surprise to Davis. Despite the indictment, May brought the best news Davis had received in more than a year. President Johnson had finally relented and agreed to let Mrs. Davis visit her husband in prison. She arrived by ship early on the morning of May 3, and after a six-hour wait was taken to see Davis.

Her first view was a shock. She later wrote that she found "the bed so infested with insects as to give a perceptible odor to the room." She said she almost cried as she first saw his "shrunken form and glassy eyes."[172]

Mrs. Davis was allowed to stay at the fort, setting up housekeeping in a separate casement inside the fort. Eventually, she was allowed to spend evenings with her husband.

In late May, Varina Davis decided to go to Washington to petition President Johnson for her husband's release. To her surprise, Johnson received her warmly, but quickly explained that his own political problems prevented him from securing the release of Davis.

Johnson said the radical Republicans were seeking any excuse to remove him from office, and releasing Davis would give them that reason. He told Mrs. Davis that her husband could petition for a pardon, but Mrs. Davis knew that he would never do that.

On June 5, Davis' attorneys petitioned the courts to bring his case to trial quickly. Two days later the government countered that Davis was not in the court's jurisdiction, but was being held "under order of the President, signed by the Secretary of War." The attorneys then asked that Davis be released on bail, but the request was quickly rejected.

Federal officials decided to bring Davis to trial in October, with Supreme Court Chief Justice Salmon P. Chase presiding.

At the end of summer, Miles was replaced as fort commander by the more humane Brigadier General Henry S. Burton, who allowed Davis and his wife to set up a small apartment and live together for the first time since they had fled Richmond, seventeen months earlier.

Davis began to receive a stream of visitors, including former President Franklin Pierce, whom Davis had served as Secretary of War. His health, however, remained fragile. As he slept, his wife would feel his pulse to make sure he was still alive.

Davis was looking forward to his October trial, sure of vindication and quick release, but shortly before the trial was to begin, the Federal authorities again announced a postponement. The trial would be delayed until the spring of 1867, which meant Davis would have to spend another cruel winter in prison.

In the north, meanwhile, sympathy had continued to increase for Davis and reached a crucial stage on November 9, when Horace Greeley, editor of the *New York Tribune*, wrote an editorial calling on the Federal government to release Davis. The strong editorial concluded by saying, "A great government may deal sternly with the offenders, but not meanly; it cannot afford to seem unwilling to repair an obvious wrong."[173]

Christmas passed and a new year began, and Davis remained in jail. Varina Davis did manage to recruit a vital ally, John W. Garrett, president of the Baltimore and Ohio Railroad. Garrett had played a large role in moving Union troops throughout the war, and Secretary Stanton was clearly in his debt.

Garrett agreed to travel to Washington and see Stanton to plead Davis' case. He found Stanton at his home, sick in bed. The two argued briefly, and finally Stanton agreed not to put up further resistance to the release of Davis.

140

Jefferson Davis Is Imprisoned

The ordeal was nearly over. Raising the bail proved relatively easy, with Greeley and Cornelius Vanderbilt each pledging to contribute.

On Friday, May 10, exactly two years after Davis was captured, a writ was handed to fort commander Burton instructing him to turn Davis over to the United States District Court three days later.

On Saturday, Davis left the fort for the first time in nearly two years for the river journey to Richmond. Davis spent the night in the Spotswood Hotel, occupying the same rooms he used when he first arrived in Richmond six years earlier.

At eleven a.m. on Monday, Jefferson Davis appeared in court. After some preliminary legal matters were dispensed with, bail was fixed at $100,000, and the bail papers were quickly signed.

Davis left Virginia, and after a brief stop in New York, traveled to Canada, where he received a warm reception.

From there, he went to England, then to France. In Paris, he was invited to see Napoleon III, but turned down the invitation, still bitter over France's refusal to aid the Confederacy.

He returned to the United States, but had a difficult time adjusting to civilian life. He had spent most of his life in government service and was not prepared to run a business. A large insurance company he headed soon failed and a second attempt in business also ended badly. But as Reconstruction dragged on, his standing in the South rose. It had been Davis who accurately predicted the fate of the South if the war was lost. Davis turned to writing, seeking to justify his own conduct of the war and defend his government. He died in 1889.

References

CHAPTER I

1. Downey & Manarin, *The Wartime Papers of R.E. Lee*, p. 911.
2. Eaton, *History of the Southern Confederacy*, p. 261.
3. Downey & Manarin, *The Wartime Papers of R.E. Lee*, p. 909.
4. Stillwell, *John Cabell Breckinridge, p. 131.*
5. Downey & Manarin, *The Wartime Papers of R.E. Lee*, p. 884.
6. Sandburg, *Abraham Lincoln: The War Years*, pp. 210–211.
7. Thomas, *The Confederate Nation*, p. 292.
8. Yearns, *The Confederate Congress*, p. 10.
9. Davis, *To Appomattox, Nine April Days*, pp. 10–11.
10. Meade, *Judah P. Benjamin, Confederate Statesman*, p. 311.
11. Davis, *To Appomattox, Nine April Days*, pp. 10–11.
12. Davis, *Jefferson Davis, Ex-President of the Confederate States*, pp. 575–577.
13. Wooster, *The Secession Conventions of the South*, p. 149.
14. Yearns, *The Confederate Congress*, p. 13.
15. Downey, *Experiment in Rebellion*, p. 398.
16. Davis, *To Appomattox, Nine April Days*, p. 13.
17. Pickett, *Pickett and His Men*, p. 386.
18. Downey & Manarin, *The Wartime Papers of R.E. Lee*, p. 978.
19. Foote, *The Civil War: A Narrative; Red River to Appomattox*, p. 862.

20. Davis, *The Rise and Fall of the Confederate Government*, p. 749.
21. Downey & Manarin, *The Wartime Papers of R.E. Lee*, p. 924.
22. *Ibid.*, p. 925.
23. Reagan, *Memoirs with Special Reference to Secession and the Civil War*, p. 196.
24. Mallory, *The Last Days of the Confederate Government*, p. 100.
25. Downey & Manarin, *The Wartime Papers of R.E. Lee*, p. 986.
26. Davis, *To Appomattox, Nine April Days*, p. 96.
27. Mallory, *Last Days of the Confederate Government*, p. 100.
28. Davis, *To Appomattox, Nine April Days*, pp. 15, 112-114.
29. Downey & Manarin, *The Wartime Papers of R.E. Lee*, pp. 927-928.
30. *Ibid.*, p. 928.
31. Davis, *To Appomattox, Nine April Days*, pp. 113-114.
32. Foote, *The Civil War: A Narrative; Red River to Appomattox*, p. 887.
33. Southern Historical Society Papers, *Evacuation of Richmond*, 268.
34. Davis, *To Appomattox, Nine April Days*, p. 114-115.
35. Foote, *The Civil War: A Narrative; Red River to Appomattox*, p. 881.
36. Strode, *Jefferson Davis, Tragic Hero*, p. 169.
37. Davis, *To Appomattox, Nine April Days*, p. 108-110.
38. *Ibid.*, p. 101.
39. Downey, *Experiment in Rebellion*, p. 406.

CHAPTER II

40. Wesley, *The Collapse of the Confederacy*, p. 294.
41. Wise, *End of an Era*, pp. 414-415.
42. Mallory, *Last Days of the Confederate Government*, p. 102.
43. Wise, *End of an Era*, p. 415.
44. Mallory, *The Last Days of the Confederate Government*, p. 105.
45. *Ibid.*, p. 104.
46. Meade, *Judah P. Benjamin, Confederate Statesman*, p. 3.
47. Durkin, *Stephen R. Mallory*, p. 350.
48. Coulter, *The Confederate States of America*, p. 299.
49. Harrison Family Papers, Library of Congress *Breckinridge to Davis, Harrison Papers*, April 8, 1865.

CHAPTER III

50. Davis, *Rise and Fall of the Confederate Government*, pp. 677-678.
51. *Ibid.*, p. 676.

References

52. Davis, *Jefferson Davis, Ex-President of the Confederate States*, p. 585.
53. Davis, *Rise and Fall of the Confederate Government*, p. 676.
54. Brubaker, *The Last Capital*, p. 32.
55. Davis, Quoted in *Rise and Fall of the Confederate Government*, pp. 677–678.
56. Foote, *The Civil War: A Narrative; Red River to Appomattox*, p. 942.
57. Downey & Manarin, *The Wartime Papers of R.E. Lee*, p. 936.
58. Rowland, *Jefferson Davis, Constitutionalist*, vol. 6, p. 532.
59. Mallory, *The Last Days of the Confederate Government*, p. 105.
60. *Confederate Veteran*, p. 451.
61. Rowland, *Jefferson Davis, Constitutionalist*, vol. 6, p. 534.
62. Stern, *An End to Valor*, p. 233.
63. Downey & Manarin, *The Wartime Papers of R.E. Lee*, pp. 931–932.
64. McFeely, *Grant: A Biography*, p. 217.
65. Downey & Manarin, *The Wartime Papers of R.E. Lee*, p. 932.
66. Wise, *The End of an Era*, p. 446.
67. Downey & Manarin, *The Wartime Papers of R.E. Lee*, p. 933.
68. Lee, *General Lee*, p. 377.
69. Downey & Manarin, *The Wartime Papers of R.E. Lee*, p. 931.
70. Rowland, *Jefferson Davis, Constitutionalist*, vol. 6, p. 541.
71. Brubaker, *The Last Capital*, pp. 50–51.
72. *Ibid.*, p. 54.
73. Mallory, *The Last Days of the Confederate Government*, p. 107.

CHAPTER IV

74. Butler, *Judah P. Benjamin*, p. 314.
75. Brubaker, *The Last Capital*, pp. 57, 59.
76. Mallory, *The Last Days of the Confederate Government*, p. 107.
77. Harrison, *The Capture of Jefferson Davis*, p. 132.
78. *Confederate Veteran*, p. 451.
79. Downey & Manarin, *The Wartime Papers of R.E. Lee*, pp. 934–935.
80. Parker, *Recollections of a Naval Officer*, p. 355.

CHAPTER V

81. Mallory, *The Last Days of the Confederate Government*, p. 107.
82. *Ibid.*
83. Harrison, *The Capture of Jefferson Davis*, p. 132.
84. Mallory, *The Last Days of the Confederate Government*, p. 240.
85. *Ibid.*, pp. 107, 239.

86. Foote, *The Civil War: A Narrative; Red River to Appomattox*, p. 966.
87. *Ibid.*, 967.
88. Davis, *The Rise and Fall of the Confederate Government*, p. 680.
89. Hanna, *Flight into Oblivion*, p. 35.
90. Downey & Manarin, *The Wartime Papers of R.E. Lee*, pp. 935–938.
91. Foote, *The Civil War: A Narrative; Red River to Appomattox*, p. 968.
92. Reagan, *Memoirs with Special Reference to Secession and the Civil War*, p. 199.
93. Mallory, *The Last Days of the Confederate Government*, pp. 146, 240–242.
94. Foote, *The Civil War: A Narrative; Red River to Appomattox*, p. 969.
95. Rowland, *Jefferson Davis, Constitutionalist*, vol. 6, p. 545.
96. Chestnut, *A Diary from Dixie*, pp. 519–520.
97. Davis, *Jefferson Davis, Ex-President of the Confederate States*, pp. 611–612.
98. Hanna, *Flight into Oblivion*, p. 34.

CHAPTER VI

99. Harrison, *The Capture of Jefferson Davis*, p. 134.
100. *Ibid.*, p. 135.
101. Dowd, *Life of Zebulon B. Vance*, pp. 485–486.
102. Harrison, *The Capture of Jefferson Davis*, p. 136.
103. Davis, *Jefferson Davis, Ex-President of the Confederate States*, pp. 627–628.
104. Hanna, *Flight into Oblivion*, pp. 82–83.
105. Mallory, *The Last Days of the Confederate Government*, p. 244.
106. Rowland, *Jefferson Davis, Constitutionalist*, vol. 6, p. 552.
107. *Ibid.*, pp. 559–560.
108. Downey & Manarin, *The Wartime Papers of R.E. Lee*, pp. 938–939.

CHAPTER VII

109. Hanna, *Flight into Oblivion*, p. 48; *The Capture of Jefferson Davis*, p. 137.
110. Rowland, *Jefferson Davis, Constitutionalist*, pp. 580–581, and 572–573.
111. Foote, *The Civil War: A Narrative; Red River to Appomattox*, p. 1002.
112. Rowland, *Jefferson Davis, Constitutionalist*, vol. 6, p. 566.
113. Downey, *Experiment in Rebellion*, p. 418.
114. Davis, *Jefferson Davis*, Ex-President of the Confederate States, p. 612, 613–614.

References

115. Hanna, *Flight into Oblivion*, pp. 55, 56.
116. Harrison, *The Capture of Jefferson Davis*, p. 137.
117. Rowland, *Jefferson Davis, Constitutionalist*, vol. 6, pp. 157–158.
118. Parker, *Recollections of a Naval Officer*, p. 364.
119. Johnson & Buel, *Battles and Leaders of the Civil War*, p. 764.
120. *Ibid.*, pp. 764–765.
121. Rowland, *Jefferson Davis, Constitutionalist*, vol. VI, p. 586.

CHAPTER VIII

122. Parker, *Recollections of a Naval Officer*, p. 367.
123. Rowland, *Jefferson Davis, Constitutionalist*, vol. 6, p. 589.
124. Davis, *Rise and Fall of the Confederate Government*, p. 695.
125. Meade, *Judah P. Benjamin*, p. 362.
126. *Official Records of the Union and Confederate Navies*, p. 1278.
127. Davis, *Jefferson Davis, Ex-President of the Confederate States*, p. 616.
128. McElroy, *Jefferson Davis: The Unreal and the Real*, p. 502.
129. Reagan, *Memoirs with Special Reference to Secession and the Civil War*, p. 217.
130. Harrison, *The Capture of Jefferson Davis*, p. 141.
131. Reagan, *Memoirs with Special Reference to Secession and the Civil War*, p. 220.
132. Harrison, *The Capture of Jefferson Davis*, p. 142.
133. Davis, *The Rise and Fall of the Confederate Government*, p. 702.
134. McElroy, *Jefferson Davis: The Unreal and the Real*, p. 512.
135. Downey, *Experiment in Rebellion*, p. 428.
136. *Ibid.*, pp. 427, 428.
137. Foote, *The Civil War: A Narrative; Red River to Appomattox*, pp. 1010–1012.

CHAPTER IX

138. Davis, *Breckinridge: Statesman, Soldier, Symbol*, p. 400.
139. Hanna, *Flight into Oblivion*, p. 104.
140. Davis, *Breckinridge, Statesman, Soldier, Symbol*, p. 527.
141. Hanna, *Flight into Oblivion*, p. 131.
142. Dickinson, *Dickinson and His Men*, p. 225.
143. Davis, *Breckinridge, Statesman, Soldier, Symbol*, p. 531.
144. Hanna, *Flight into Oblivion*, p. 144.
145. *Ibid*, pp. 155–159.
146. *Ibid.*, p. 165.

147. Wood, *Escape of the Confederate Secretary of War*, p. 115.
148. *Ibid.*, pp. 115–117.
149. Hanna, *Flight into Oblivion*, p. 182.

CHAPTER X

150. Reagan, *Memoirs with Special Reference to Secession and Civil War*, p. 211.
151. Wood, *Escape of the Confederate Secretary of War*, p. 110.
152. Butler, *Judah P. Benjamin*, p. 364.
153. Hanna, *Flight into Oblivion*, pp. 201, 203–205.
154. Pierce, *Judah P. Benjamin*, p. 364.
155. Hanna, *Flight into Oblivion*, p. 221.

CHAPTER XI

156. Durkin, quoted passages in this chapter are from *Stephen R. Mallory*, pp. 344–345, 347–348, 356, 363, 365, 373
157. Southern History Association, *West Florida Commercial*, April 23, 1869.
158. *Ibid.*

CHAPTER XII

159. Pierce, *Judah P. Benjamin*, pp. 7–8.
160. Meade, *Judah P. Benjamin, Confederate Statesman*, p. 29.
161. Hendrick, *Statesmen of the Lost Cause*, p. 154.
162. *Ibid*, p. 167.

CHAPTER XIII

163. Davis, *Jefferson Davis, Ex-President of the Confederate States*, p. 648.
164. Craven, *The Prison Life of Jefferson Davis*, pp. 35, 36–37.
165. Strode, *Jefferson Davis, Tragic Hero*, p. 231.
166. Craven, *The Prison Life of Jefferson Davis*, p. 41.
167. *Ibid.*, p. 88.
168. *Ibid.*, p. 90.
169. Rowland, *Jefferson Davis, Constitutionalist*, vol. 7, p. 49.
170. Strode, *Jefferson Davis, Tragic Hero*, p. 273.

References

171. *Ibid.*, p. 279.
172. Davis, *Jefferson Davis, Ex-President of the Confederate States*, p. 759.
173. Strode, *Jefferson Davis*, Tragic Hero, p. 297.

Bibliography

Periodicals

Danville, Va., *Weekly Register*, April 7, 1865 and May 17, 1865.

Harrison, Burton N., *The Capture of Jefferson Davis*, Century Magazine, XXVII, 130–145, November, 1883.

Haw, Joseph R., *The Last of the C.S. Ordnance Department*, Confederate Veteran, XXXIV, 450–452, December, 1926.

Mallory, Stephen R., *The Last Days of the Confederate Government*, McClure's Magazine, XVI, 99–107, December, 1900 and 239–248, January, 1901.

Swallow, W.H., *Retreat of the Confederate Government from Richmond to the Gulf*, Magazine of American History, XV, 596–608, June, 1886.

Wamsley, J.E., *The Last Meeting of the Confederate Cabinet*, Mississippi Valley Historical Review, VI, 336–349, December, 1919.

West Florida Commercial (Pensacola), April 23, 1869.

Wood, John Taylor, *Escape of the Confederate Secretary of War*, Century Magazine, XLVII, 110–123, November, 1893.

Southern Historical Society Papers, Richmond

The True Story of the Capture of Jefferson Davis, V, 97–126, March, 1878.

The Last Days of the Confederate Treasury, IX, 542–556, December, 1881.

Last Letters and Telegrams of the Confederacy, XII, 97–105, March, 1884.

The Evacuation of Richmond, XIII, 247–59, January, 1885.

Retreat of the Cabinet, XLI, 96–101, December, 1898.

Cabinet Meeting at Charlotte, XLI, 61–67, September, 1916.

Southern History Association

President Davis' Last Official Meeting, V, 291–299, July, 1901.

Books

Butler, Pierce, *Judah P. Benjamin*, George W. Jacobs & Co., Philadelphia, Pa., 1907.

Brubaker, John H., III, *The Last Capital*, Danville Museum of Fine Arts and History, Danville, Va., 1979.

Chestnut, Mary, *A Diary from Dixie*, Ben Ames Williams, editor, Harvard University Press, Cambridge, Mass., 1962.

Bibliography

Coulter, Merton E., *The Confederate States of America*, Louisiana State University Press, Baton Rouge, La., 1950.

Craven, John J., *The Prison Life of Jefferson Davis*, Carleton Publishers, New York, 1866.

Davis, Burke, *To Appomattox, Nine April Days, 1865*, Holt, Rinehart and Winston, New York, 1958.

Davis, Jefferson, *The Rise and Fall of the Confederate Government*, D. Appleton & Co., New York, 1881, 2 vols.

Davis, Varina Howell, *Jefferson Davis, Ex-President of the Confederate States, A Memoir*, Belford Co., New York, 1890, 2 vols.

Davis, William C., *Breckinridge: Statesman, Soldier, Symbol*, Louisiana State University Press, Baton Rouge, La., 1974.

Dickinson, Mary Elizabeth, *Dickinson and His Men*, University of Florida Press, Gainesville, Fla., 1962.

Dowd, Clement, *Life of Zebulon B. Vance*, Observer Printing & Publishing House, Charlotte, N.C., 1897.

Downey, Clifford, *Experiment in Rebellion*, Doubleday & Co., New York, 1946.

_____, and Louis H. Manarin, eds, *The Wartime Papers of R.E. Lee*, Bramhall House, New York, 1961.

Johnson, R.V. and C.C. Buel, eds., *Battles and Leaders of the Civil War*, Century Co., New York, 1884, 4 vols.

Durkin, S.J., *Stephen R. Mallory*, University of North Carolina Press, Chapel Hill, N.C., 1954.

Eaton, Clement, A *History of the Southern Confederacy*, Macmillan Publishing Co., 1954.

Bibliography

Foote, Shelby, *The Civil War, A Narrative; Red River to Appomattox*, Random House, New York, 1974.

Hanna, A.J., *Flight into Oblivion*, Johnson Publishing Co., Richmond, Va., 1938.

Hendrick, Burton J., *Statesmen of the Lost Cause*, Little, Brown & Co., Boston, 1938.

Lee, Fitzhugh, *General Lee*, D. Appleton & Co., New York, 1894.

McElroy, Robert, *Jefferson Davis, The Unreal and the Real*, Harper & Bros., New York, 1937, 2 vols.

McFeely, William S., *Grant: A Biography*, W.W. Norton & Co., New York, 1981.

Meade, Robert D., *Judah P. Benjamin, Confederate Statesman*, Oxford University Press, New York, 1943.

Moore, Albert M., *Conscritpion and Conflict in the Confederacy*, Hillary House Publishers, New York, 1963.

Nevins, Allan, *The War for the Union: The Organized War to Victory, 1864–1865*, Charles Scribner's Sons, New York, 1971.

Parker, William H., *Recollections of a Naval Officer*, Charles Scribner's Sons, New York, 1883.

Patrick, Rembert W., *The Fall of Richmond*, Louisiana State University Press, Baton Rouge, La., 1960.

————, *Jefferson Davis and His Cabinet*, Louisiana State University Press, Baton Rouge, La., 1944.

Pickett, La Salle, *Pickett and His Men*, J.B. Lippincott Co., Philadelphia, 1913.

Reagan, John H., *Memoirs with Special Reference to Secession and the Civil War*, Neale Publishing Co., New York, 1906.

Bibliography

Rowland, Dunbar, *Jefferson Davis, Constitutionalist*, Mississippi Department of Archives and History, Jackson, Miss., 1923, 10 vols.

Sandburg, Carl, *Abraham Lincoln; The War Years*, Harcourt, Brace and Co., New York, 1939.

Stern, Phillip V., *End to Valor*, Houghton Mifflin Co., Boston, 1958.

Stillwell, Lucille, *John Cabell Breckinridge*, Caxton Printers Ltd., Caldwell, Idaho, 1936.

Strode, Hudson, *Jefferson Davis, Tragic Hero*, Harcourt, Brace & World, 1964.

Thomas, Emory M., *The Confederate Nation*, Harper & Row, New York, 1979.

Todd, Richard Cecil, *Confederate Finance*, University of Georgia Press, Athens, Ga., 1954.

Wise, John S., *The End of an Era*, Houghton Mifflin Co., Boston, 1902.

Wesley, Charles H., *The Collapse of the Confederacy*, Associated Publishers, Washington, D.C., 1937.

Wooster, Ralph A., *The Secession Conventions of the South*, Princeton University Press, Princeton, N.J., 1962.

Yearns, Wilfrd Buck, *The Confederate Congress*, University of Georgia Press, Athens, Ga., 1960.

Manuscripts

Clark, Micajah H., Papers, Library of Congress.

Davis, Jefferson, Collection, Library of Congress.

Bibliography

Harrison, Family Papers, Library of Congress, includes papers of
    Burton Harrison.

Stanton, Edwin M., Papers, Library of Congress.

Index

A

Abbeville, South Carolina, 66, 73, 79, 81, 84, 88, 94, 100
Amelia Court House, 13, 40, 59
Anderson, Abner, 38
Anderson, General R.H., 17, 60
Appomattox, Virginia, 17, 44, 51, 58
Appomattox Court House, 42, 45, 59, 61, 62
Army of Northern Virginia, 3, 41, 42, 43, 52, 59, 62, 75
Athens, Georgia, 93
Atlanta, Georgia, 55, 80, 81, 123
Augusta, Georgia, 84, 99, 137
Augusta Constitutionalist, 72

B

Baltimore, Maryland, 100

Baltimore and Ohio Railroad, 140
Bank of North Carolina, 82
Barringer, Judge Victor C., 72
Bates, Mr. L.F., 73
Beauregard, General P.G.T., 48, 57, 58, 59, 63, 64, 74
Benjamin, Judah P.: aboard train to Danville, 27; background, 28–31; in Danville, 37; helps write proclamation, 38; leaves Greensboro, 67–68; in Charlotte, 72–73; destroys government papers, 87; sought by Wood, 107; escape through Florida, 117–120; sought by George Davis, 121; returns to England, 129–130; career in England, 131
Benjamin, Mrs. Judah P., 131
Bermuda, 80
Bimini, 120
Boston, Massachusetts, 131, 133
Bragg, General Braxton, 26
Bratton, James Rufus, 84

157

Index

Index

Hawkinsville, Georgia, 95
Hendra, John, 15
High Point, North Carolina, 69
Hill, Benjamin, 123, 124
Hoge, Dr. Moses, 27, 37, 41
Howell, Mrs. Maggie, 6
Hunter, Robert M.T., 29

I

Indian River, 92, 109
Interstate Commerce Commission, 132
Irving, William, 13
Irwinsville, Georgia, 95

J

Jacksonville, Georgia, 105
Jamestown, North Carolina, 68
Jetersville, Virginia, 60
Johnson, General B.R., 60
Johnson, Andrew, 71–72, 98, 125
Johnston, John M., 37
Johnston, General Joseph, 2, 35, 37, 48, 51, 52, 63–64, 71, 72, 74, 78, 79, 82
Johnston, Colonel William, 20, 71, 94, 95
Jones, James, 6, 95

K

Kercheval, Andrew, 50
Kershaw, General Joseph, 60
Key West Florida, 31, 92
Knights Key, Florida, 119

L

La Grange, Georgia, 123
Lane, Mrs. Thomas, 121
Lee, General Custis, 60
Lee, General Fitz, 61
Lee, General Robert E.: rejects plan for merging armies, 2; named general in chief, 3; comment on Five Forks, 9; warns Davis, 10; tells Breckinridge he cannot hold position, 11–12; tells Davis evacuation should begin, 12; message to Breckinridge about evacuation, 13; on recruiting Negro troops, 16; message to Davis on evacuation, 17–18; on outcome of war, 21; meets Breckinridge, 35; advice on conduct of war, 40; seeks terms from Grant, 42; message to Grant, 43; seeks suspension of hostilities, 44; surrenders his army, 45; issues final general order, 51–52, letter to Davis explaining surrender, 59–62; mentioned, 64, 66; letter to Davis, 75–76; mentioned, 78, 79, 89
Lee, General W.H.F., 60
Leovy, Colonel H.J., 118
Leovy, Mrs. Henry, 92
Lexington, North Carolina, 69, 70
Lincoln, Abraham, 1, 40, 64, 69, 71, 73, 98, 101
Live Oak, Florida, 106
Lieber, Francis, 138
Lomax, General Lunsford, 35
London, 131
Longstreet, General James, 60, 61, 62
Lubbock, Governor Francis, 20, 37, 97
Lynchburg, Virginia, 45, 60, 61, 62

161

Index

Philbrook, Walter, 18, 19
Pickett, General George, 4, 9, 16–17, 60
Pierce, Franklin, 140
Pritchard, Colonel B.D., 96–97

R

Raleigh, North Carolina, 57
Reagan, John H.: awaits word from Lee, 11; delivers message to Davis, 12; aboard train from Richmond, 26; background, 28; sets up post office in Danville, 41; meets with Johnston, 69–70; meets with Sherman, 71; arrives in Charlotte, 77; comments on treaty with Sherman, 78; named treasury secretary, 83; comments to Davis, 87; pays midshipmen, 88; decides to remain with Davis, 89, 93; captured, 97; in prison, 117, 121; visits Mallory in prison, 127; later life, 131–132, moved to Fort Warren, 133
Richmond, Virginia, 2, 4, 7, 8, 9, 13, 14, 18, 20, 21, 23, 26, 27, 38, 47, 55, 59, 63, 75, 115, 120, 138, 141
Richmond Evening Whig, 72
Russell, Corporal Richard, 108, 113, 116

S

St. Johns River, 109
St. Pauls Church, 12–14, 138
St. Peter's Church, 77
Salisbury, North Carolina, 70

Sarasota Bay, Florida, 119
Saunders, Elizabeth, 22
Saundersville, Georgia, 93
Savannah, Georgia, 99, 132, 135, 137
Schley, George, 137
Scott, Walter, 70
Selma, Alabama, 79
Seminole Indians, 111
Semmes, Admiral Raphael, 38, 40, 41, 46
Sheridan, General Phillip, 16
Sherman, General William, 2, 37, 48, 55, 69, 71, 73, 77, 78, 79, 81, 92, 103
Slaves, 3
Smith, General Kirby, 69, 72, 93, 107, 120
Smith, Governor William, 48
Smithfield, North Carolina, 58
Southern Express Company, 73
Springs, Colonel A.B., 83
Stanton, Edwin, 79, 82, 101, 117, 125, 127, 137, 138, 140
Stephens, Alexander, 99, 121, 133
Stevens, General Walter, 12
Stoneman, General George, 10, 35, 55
Sutherlin, Major W.T., 37, 45
Sutherlin, Mrs. W.T., 45, 48

T

Tallahassee, Florida, 93
Taylor, Zachery, 109
Thorburn, Colonel Charles, 92, 107
Tomlinson, A.R., 9
Toombs, Robert A., 29
Trenholm, George, 14, 26, 32, 37, 49, 56, 68, 72, 83, 117, 132
Trenholm, Mrs. George, 37